SERMONS ON SPECIAL DAYS

D1056647

WILLIAM D. WATLEY

SERMONS ON SPECIAL DAYS

PREACHING
THROUGH
THE YEAR
IN THE
BLACK
CHURCH

Judson Press ® Valley Forge

SERMONS ON SPECIAL DAYS

Copyright © 1987
Judson Press, Valley Forge, PA 19482-0851

All rights reserved. No part of this publication may be reproduced, stored in a retrieval system, or transmitted in any form or by any means, electronic, mechanical, photocopying, recording, or otherwise, without the prior permission of the copyright owner, except for brief quotations included in a review of the book.

Unless otherwise indicated, all Scripture quotations are taken from the Revised Standard Version of the Bible, copyrighted 1946, 1952, © 1971, 1973 by the Division of Christian Education of the National Council of the Churches of Christ in the U.S.A., and used by permission. Other quotations are taken from *The Holy Bible*, King James Version; and *The Living Bible*. Tyndale House Publishers, Wheaton, Ill. Used by permission.

Library of Congress Cataloging-in-Publication Data

Watley, William D.
    Sermons on special days.

      1. Occasional sermons.   2. Church year sermons.
3. Sermons, American—Afro-American authors.   I. Title.
BV4254.2.W37   1987   252'.0783   87-4191
ISBN 0-8170-1089-0

The name JUDSON PRESS is registered as a trademark in the U.S. Patent Office. Printed in the U.S.A.

Acknowledgments

Books are never the work of one person even when they bear the name of a single author. Behind every author stands a number of persons, "a great cloud of witnesses," who have assisted indirectly or directly through inference, influence, direct contact, or technical assistance. This book is no exception. I am thankful for the privilege of acknowledging some of those whose influence and assistance have made this book possible.

I am grateful to God for my grandmother, the late Mrs. Fannie Thomas, affectionately known to her family as Mama Fannie, who taught me from "the rocking of my cradle" to reach farther than my grasp. Like so many mothers and grandmothers, her formal education was meager, but the profundity of her wisdom was matched only by the depth of her faith, the power of her determination, and her sacrificial love for her children. I am pleased to dedicate this book to the memory of Mama Fannie.

The Reverend Harvey L. Vaughn, Sr., former Presiding Elder of the African Methodist Episcopal (AME) Church of the Missouri Conference, who licensed me to preach, and the Rev. E. Woody Hall, formerly of Kansas City, Missouri, a prince among preachers whose insights into the Scriptures I shall never forget, have both passed from labor to reward since the preparation of my first book of sermons. I pause to remember them also.

I am grateful to all of those who have assisted me directly in the production of this book. Thanks to my sister and friend Mrs. Carolyn Scavella who again has served as my first reader and redactor, also, not only for her technical assistance but for the gift of her insights. I am grateful to my administrative assistant at St. James AME Church, Rev. Marie Russell, who had the onerous task of deciphering my handwriting and typing the manuscript. Mrs. Mary Wills, another faithful member of St. James, also gave some early typing assistance.

This is my third publication by Judson Press, and I have enjoyed the relationship that I have developed with the staff, particularly Laura Alden, Phyllis Frantz, and Michelle Esbenshade.

I am grateful to my bishop, the Right Reverend Frank C. Cummings, who has encouraged and supported me in this ministry of the written word. I continue to praise God for the membership of St. James AME Church in Newark, New Jersey, who have been generous with their praise and sparing with their criticism as I have labored to serve them as shepherd.

Last but certainly not least, I am grateful to God for the love of those who know this preacher better than any who might hear him or read his works because they live with him—my wife, Muriel, my children, Jennifer and Matthew, and my mother-in-law, Mrs. Noretta Vaught. They are not only integral to my personal life but to my ministry as well. They are patient with my weekly preparation time at home and prayerful as they sit in the pew.

Happy and fortunate are those of us whose lives are blessed with family, friends, and others who care enough to give of themselves so that we might grow.

William D. Watley

Contents

Business as Usual Is No Longer Acceptable

Luke 17:26-29

Jesus had essentially one sermon. Everything he did and said revolved around that one message which was "the kingdom of heaven is at hand." He reminded those who exercised power of any kind on earth that they did not have the last word. He informed them that with his coming and in his person God was about to do something refreshing and radical, something which would be liberating and which would challenge old ways of doing and thinking about things. Jesus came to call the powers that be into question and put them on notice that business as they had been doing it, business as they knew it, business as usual, was no longer acceptable.

Thus, every miracle he performed established his supremacy over forces and systems which heretofore believed they had the last word regarding the human predicament. Every time Jesus healed a sick person he demonstrated that sickness and disease do not have ultimate control of the body because God's promise, God's deliverance, God's power, and God's comfort were present in Jesus. Every time he rebuked a demon he demonstrated that we do not have to live in fear of either the unknown or of evil because there is no evil power in hell, or earth, or sky which can keep one of God's children down. Every time he calmed a storm, every time he multiplied a piece of bread, every time he walked on a wave of water, he showed that nature was not in control, he was. Every time he chose to reinterpret a religious tradition he showed that even the law and the prophets found their fulfillment in him. Jesus came to declare that a new day was dawning, that God was already at work, and that business as usual, priorities as usual, living as usual were no longer acceptable.

The Pharisees, with their vested interests, came to Jesus to ask him about this new kingdom that would change every familiar thing. Whether in the church or community, those with vested interests in keeping things as they are are always the ones most concerned about change. After all, those with vested interests believe that they personally have the most to lose by change. The Pharisees came to Jesus to inquire about this new kingdom. When would it come? How would it come? What would be the signs of its coming? Jesus informed them that the kingdom would come in the same way that the rain fell from heaven in the days of Noah and the fire fell from heaven in the days of Lot. The kingdom would not come without warning because God always gives his children a warning, but people would not pay attention to the warning that was given. For if there was one thing clear about Noah and Lot it was that nobody took them seriously. Nobody believed what Noah said about the flood. And so all the while that Noah was building the ark and preparing for the flood, all the while that God was speaking to Noah, all the while that Noah preached God's message of repentance, righteousness, and judgment, the people ate and they drank, they married and were given in marriage. They did business as usual even as the flood came and destroyed them all.

The situation surrounding the ancient cities of Sodom and Gomorrah was even more critical. Throughout biblical history the names of Sodom and Gomorrah have been associated with wickedness, lewdness, and decadence. The sins of Sodom and Gomorrah were so hideous and so many that they stirred the wrath of a righteous God, and the destruction of these two towns became imminent. The people of Sodom and Gomorrah had become hopelessly mired in their transgressions. Sin is an addictive habit, and it is possible to become so controlled by it that but for the blood of Jesus one becomes irretrievably lost and bound. The people of Sodom and Gomorrah had done wrong for so long that they believed that they could get away with doing wrong forever. There comes a time, however, when heaven's patience with wrongdoing refuses to be tried any longer. The people of Sodom and Gomorrah continued doing business as usual, eating and drinking, buying and selling, planting and building, not believing that time was running out for them.

The plan for solving the Sodom and Gomorrah problem was revealed to Abraham, God's friend. Abraham said to the Lord, "I know that Sodom and Gomorrah are wicked places deserving of divine wrath, but there are some good people there. Will you destroy the city if I can find fifty righteous people there?" Let us never forget that every Sodom and Gomorrah has some good people. God's friends are found everywhere, even in Sodom and Gomorrah. A preacher once told me that even in the worst of churches God always has an angel or two in the membership who truly love the Lord, love the church, and who will try to work with the preacher. Even in the most corrupt situations there are always one or two good people, and we wonder what they are doing there. They are there because God is never left without a witness even in the most hopeless situations.

Abraham could not find fifty righteous people so he asked God if the cities could be spared for the sake of forty-five. A few people who really love God can go a long way toward redeeming any situation. When Abraham couldn't find forty-five, he went out in search of forty. When Abraham couldn't find forty, he searched for thirty; and when he couldn't find thirty, he searched for twenty. Not only could he not find twenty, he couldn't find even ten. All the while the people of Sodom and Gomorrah continued to do business as usual— eating and drinking, buying and selling, planting and building. All this time as Abraham negotiated with God not on his own behalf, but on behalf of the people of those towns; all the time he sought for a representative number of righteous persons so that the city could be saved from destruction, the people of Sodom and Gomorrah continued doing business as usual—eating and drinking, buying and selling, planting and building. Word must have gotten around about what Abraham was doing. He could not have conducted the extensive search that he did without persons being alerted, and yet they chose to conduct themselves as usual—eating and drinking, buying and selling, planting and building. They were on the very eve of destruction. One would have thought that being forewarned they would have been forearmed, and yet they chose to do business as usual—eating and drinking, buying and selling, planting and building.

On the eve of the destruction of Sodom and Gomorrah, two angels dressed as men came to visit Lot, the only righteous friend of God in Sodom. A group of inhabitants of Sodom, acting their usual crass selves, tried to attack them but were stricken blind. That next morning the angels told Lot and his family to flee the town and not to look back. Even as they fled, and even as fire fell from heaven, in spite of their repeated warnings, the people of Sodom and Gomorrah still conducted business as usual—eating and drinking, buying and selling, planting and building.

To be sure, the story of doom is not a very pleasant one. God's work of judgment can be frightening. But as frightening as God's judgment can be, the work of sin is even more frightening. Drug addiction is frightening. Alcoholism is frightening. Violence in the home which produces battered children, battered wives, and battered husbands is frightening. Pornography is frightening. Incest is frightening. Little children being sexually abused and assaulted is frightening. Innocent children being snatched off the streets is frightening. The necessity for being constantly on guard everywhere we go is frightening. Hardly feeling safe even in our own homes is frightening. More frightening than the judgment of God which redeems and restores balance is the destructive work of sin.

What is the response of the church as it exists in the midst of the work of sin? Often it's simply business as usual—eating and drinking, buying and selling, planting and building, and that's all.

With nuclear holocaust as a possibility, we may be facing the eve of our own destruction. What is the Church doing? Business as usual—eating and drinking, buying and selling, planting and building. The possibility of war and the actuality of crime, racism, sexism, classism, inadequate housing for the poor, eroding systems of public education, hunger, poverty, and expensive health care face us every day.

Our churches must be our voice in the wider community. We must be the wayfaring voice which cries in the wilderness of hostility and indifference to represent the cause and broker the interests of those whom the demonic systems of this world have bound and hold captive. Our churches must not only safeguard our spiritual life but our economic, political, social, and cultural life as well. But what do we as churches—as preachers and as members—spend the greater part of our time doing? Business as usual—eating and drinking, buying and selling, planting and building, and that's all.

Some of us are going to lose our souls and go to hell from some church kitchen, some church choir, some church board—yes, even some church pulpit—eating and drinking, buying and selling, planting and building. Some of us are lost in an auxiliary where we can exercise a little power and control with some other folk whose thinking is just like ours, where we can work on the preacher as well as some other members, away from the mainstream of the church's life and the mission given to it by Christ. What are we doing at the club meetings to which we are devoted? Business as usual—eating and drinking, buying and selling, planting and building, and that's all. Go to some of our big church meetings, gatherings, and conventions and while the world is going to hell in a basket, what are we doing? Business as usual—eating and drinking, buying and selling, planting and building, and that's all.

Those who were lost in the days of Noah and Lot were not only lost because of the activities in which they were engaged.

There's nothing wrong with eating and drinking, buying and selling, planting and building, *per se*. Their main problem was they became so engrossed in what they were doing that they failed to take note of what God was saying to them through Abraham and Lot and what God was doing in their midst through Noah. We can become so consumed in doing our own thing in life's daily routines, so lost in our own little worlds, that we are not attuned to God's plan and purpose for our lives. We can become so caught up in our own agenda that we forget that beyond us there is a divine agenda. If our agendas are going to have any ultimate meaning, they must be brought in line with God's agenda.

Business as usual is no longer acceptable when God's work of judgment is upon us. Business as usual is no longer acceptable when injustice reigns and wickedness abounds. Business as usual is no longer acceptable when Jesus has declared that the kingdom of God is at hand.

It may not be obvious, just as it was not obvious in biblical times. After all, Jesus had only a few fishermen, a few women, some children, several influential patrons, and some common people following him. But those few were all he needed to turn the world upside down.

The world after Jesus is different than the world before him. It has been redeemed. Humanity is different than it was before Jesus. We've been liberated. We as individuals are different after Jesus comes into our lives. We've been saved. That's what the kingdom of God is—saved individuals who are part of a liberated humanity and a redeemed new world "acoming." And the redemption takes place in the midst of those who are content to eat and drink, buy and sell, and plant and build themselves into eternal damnation.

As the church, we must do more than take care of our usual business—our annual days and our annual budget. We must do more than play politics and jockey for position with each other or with the pastor. We are called to do more than eat chicken and drink punch. We are called to do more than buy and sell tickets. We are called to do more than plant our usual ideas and build our usual programs.

Jesus has called us to be the "salt of the earth" and the "light of the world." We are called to be ambassadors of the Christ who said: "The Spirit of the Lord is upon me because he has anointed me to preach good news to the poor, he has sent me to heal the brokenhearted, to preach deliverance to the captives and recovery of sight to the blind, to set at liberty those who are oppressed, to proclaim the acceptable year of the Lord" (Luke 4:18-19).

We are called to be ambassadors of Jesus, who said: "Whoever would be great among you shall be the servant" (Mark 10:43) and "Inasmuch as ye have done it to the least . . . ye did it unto me . . . Inasmuch as ye did it not unto the least, ye did it not unto me" (Matthew 25:40, 43; KJV). We are called to be ambassadors of the Christ who said: "You shall love another as I have loved you" (John 15:12); and "the kingdom of God is in you" (Luke 17:21, KJV).

It's easy to become so caught up in eating and drinking, buying and selling, planting and building—our business as we usually do it—that we stop doing or even forget to ask what God wants and wills for our lives. That is why all children of God need to stop and study themselves every now and then—take inventory of their lives and the things to which they have devoted themselves and ask, "Lord, am I doing what you want me to do?"

Some of us have been doing whatever it is we're doing for a long time. We've been thinking the same thoughts a long time and we have become comfortable. Maybe we've become too comfortable because we've even stopped asking God's direction. That's why we need to ask, "Lord, am I still doing what you want me to do?"

People tell me I'm good at what I do. I've been recognized and I've received awards for what I do. But "Lord, am I doing what you want me to do, the way you want me to do it?"

Perhaps I will be accepted by those whose goals and whose visions are as shallow as mine, but "Lord, am I doing what you want me to do?" Like Peter and John, I can stay close to the shore fishing in the shallows, but I know that you want me to launch out into broader avenues of service and discover a deeper depth and a higher height in you. That is why I need to continue to ask, "Lord, am I doing what you want me to do?"

There is only one way to be saved from the trap of business as usual and that is by surrendering our total lives to the unusual business of doing God's will. Doing God's will is not easy. Noah did it and found himself being laughed at for building a boat in the middle of the desert. But it took that experience to teach Noah that God always comes out a winner at the finishing line. Abraham did it and found himself being tested on Mt. Moriah, but Mt. Moriah showed him, like nothing else could, that God will provide. Lot did it and had to flee with his family and friends as fire came down upon Sodom. But it was only as Lot fled that he learned the lesson that the prophet Isaiah would one day articulate:"Thou will keep him in perfect peace whose mind is stayed on Thee because he trusteth in Thee" (Isaiah 26:3, KJV). Jesus did it and found himself on a cross, but it took a Calvary to demonstrate that there is no resurrection without crucifixion. Peter did it and found himself in prison, but it took prison to show him that God can open doors that no one can shut. Paul did it and found himself with a thorn in the flesh, but it took the thorn to show him that God's grace was sufficient. John did it and found himself on Patmos, but it took Patmos for him to see the new heaven and the new earth, the new Jerusalem.

Long ago Noah said it and meant it. Long ago Abraham said it and meant it. Long ago Lot said it and meant it. Long ago Jesus said it and meant it. George Stebbins said it and meant it. You and I are going to have to say it and mean it too.

> Have Thine own way, Lord! Have Thine own way!
> Thou are the Potter; I am the clay.
> Mould me and make me after thy will
> While I am waiting, yielded and still.

A Strange Glory

Hebrews 1:1–3

Throughout the New Testament Jesus is perceived as embodying and manifesting, representing and incarnating the glory of God. In the great prologue of John's Gospel, we learn that the glory of Jesus is a unique glory. It is neither the glory of a good person doing good works nor the glory of an angel or other celestial figure. Rather, it is the glory of one identified as the only Son of God. As John states: "And we beheld his glory, glory as of the only Son of the Father" (John 1:14).

In the book of Hebrews, Jesus is said to be the brightness and reflection of the glory of God. As a reflection, Jesus images God's glory as a mirror reflects and images whatever object stands before it. In other words, if you want to see what God is really like, all you have to do is look at Jesus.

As a prism refracts and breaks down the light of the sun so that its separate colors can be identified, so Jesus allows us to see at close hand the attributes of God so that we can discern the various colorations and configurations of God's character. We look at Jesus and see how justice and mercy, power and patience, righteousness and grace, majesty and meekness, all being undergirded by love, blend together to form God's character and personality. This is the theological description of God's glory which has come near to us and has been manifested in Jesus.

However, when one looks at the physical manifestation of God's glory in Jesus, it appears to be a strange glory. *Schechinah* is the word which the Old Testament uses to describe God's glory when it comes near to us. *Schechinah* means "that which dwells." It is the word used to describe the visible presence of God among men and women. In the Old Testament the physical manifestation of God's glory is usually spoken of in terms of fire and lightning, majesty and splendor. Human beings have always been dazzled and have stood in open-mouthed awe and wonder, and at times terror, as they gazed upon visible manifestations of God's glory.

When the glory of God descended upon Mt. Sinai and was manifested to the children of Israel in the wilderness, the Word tells us that there was thunder and lightning, a thick cloud, and a loud trumpet; the whole mountain shook with the presence of God. When Moses went alone upon the mountain to talk with God, the Word tells us that "the appearance of the glory of the Lord was like a devouring fire on the top of the mountain" (Exodus 24:17). When the glory of God descended upon the tent of meeting, the Word tells us that

> the cloud covered the tent of meeting and the glory of the Lord filled the tabernacle. Moses was not able to enter the tent of meeting, because the cloud abode upon it and the glory of the Lord filled the tabernacle. . . .[And] throughout their journey the cloud of the Lord was upon the tabernacle by day, and fire was in it by night, in the sight of all the house of Israel (Exodus 40: 34, 38).

When Solomon dedicated the temple the Word tells us that

> when the priests came out of the holy place [the inner sanctuary], a cloud filled the house of the Lord so that the priests could not stand to minister because of the cloud; for the glory of the Lord filled the house of the Lord" (1 Kings 8:10-12).

When Isaiah had his vision, he described the Lord seated upon a throne, high and lifted up with his train filling the temple. Above the throne stood the seraphim, each of whom had six wings—with two they covered their face, with two they covered their feet, and with two they flew. And they cried to each other, "Holy, holy, holy, is the Lord of hosts; the whole earth is full of his glory" (Isaiah 6:3). And the foundation of the temple was shaken at the voice of the one who spoke, and the house was filled with smoke.

Ezekiel described his vision of God's glory by saying that

Above the firmament, high in the sky, I saw the likeness of a throne which was in appearance like blue sapphire stones, and seated upon the throne was the likeness of a human form.

From the waist up he seemed to be glowing bronze, dazzling like fire; and from the waist down he seemed to be entirely flame, and there was a glowing halo like rainbow all around him . . . Such was the appearance of the likeness of the glory of the Lord. (Ezekiel 1:26-28, *The Living Bible*).

Such were some of the various ways that the glory of God was revealed in times past. It was revealed in cloud and smoke, fire and brightness, especially when God's presence came near to the place of worship—whether on a mountaintop, in the tent, or in the temple. Thus our text reminds us: "In many and various ways God spoke of old to our fathers by the prophets; but in these last days he has spoken to us by a Son, whom he appointed the heir of all things, through whom also he created the world. He reflects the glory of God and bears the very stamp of his nature, upholding the universe by his word of power."

One dark and dreary night a group of shepherds were keeping a lonely vigil as they watched over their flocks when, according to the Word,

the angel of the Lord came upon them and the glory of the Lord shone round about them, and they were sore afraid. And the angel said unto them, "Fear not: for behold, I bring you good tidings of great joy, which shall be to all people. For unto you is born this day in the city of David a Saviour, which is Christ the Lord. And this shall be a sign unto you: Ye shall find the babe wrapped in swaddling clothes, lying in a manger." And suddenly there was with the angel a multitude of heavenly host praising God, and saying, "Glory to God in the highest, and on earth peace, good will towards men." And it came to pass, as the angels were gone away from them into heaven, the shepherds said one to another, "Let us now go even unto Bethlehem and see this thing which is come to pass, which the Lord hath made known unto us." And they came with haste, and found Mary, and Joseph, and the babe lying in the manger (Luke 2:9-16, KJV).

They came in haste to find the Saviour who had been heralded by angels shouting "Glory!" They came to find the Saviour who was the greatest manifestation of God's glory. And what did they find? The first thing they found was a grotto where animals were kept in the back of a second-rate motel. There were no angels hovering over it or clouds surrounding it, no smoke within it, or fire or brightness radiating from it. It was just an ordinary cow barn, a regular horse stable, a plain old pig pen, a run-of-the-mill chicken coop. One would not expect to find the glory of God in a place like that. In a temple, yes; in the synagogue, sure; in the council room of the Sanhedrin, possibly; but not in an animal haven. If this was the place of God's glory, it was a strange glory.

And whom did they find? They found Mary, an ordinary handmaiden and homemaker—not the governor's or emperor's, or bishop's, or moderator's wife; not even the president of the business and professional women's league—but plain Mary. The found Joseph—not the high priest, or the governor, or the emperor, or the chairman of the board of a Fortune 500 multinational corporation—but Joseph the carpenter. Whom did they find? They found the baby Jesus. The greatest manifestation of the same God, who in times past, had spoken forth in the rolling thunder and flashes of lightning and whose presence was identified with might and majesty, was in the form of a baby. What a strange glory! One would expect the glory of this God of power, who formed the ends of the earth, to come forth like the trumpet blasts of Caesar's legions. But instead, it comes in the whimper of a child. What a strange glory!

The strange glory of Jesus' birth was manifested throughout his life. Nathaniel thought it especially strange that Nazareth, rather than Jerusalem or one of the other more prestigious towns, should be linked with the glory of the Messiah. When Philip told him that he had found the One about whom Moses wrote and the prophets preached and that He was from Nazareth, Nathaniel replied, "Can anything good come out of Nazareth?" (John 1:46). The glory of Moses and the prophets associated with Nazareth—what a strange glory.

The glory of Jesus was so strange, particularly as that glory was manifested among some of society's undesirables in a forgiving spirit and with a contrite heart, that even John the Baptist, Jesus' forerunner, was taken aback by it. John sent messengers to Jesus asking, "Are you sure that you are the one who is to come or look we for another?" The glory of God's Anointed being manifested among prostitutes and tax collectors—what a strange glory.

What was strangest of all was the way Jesus talked about death on the cross as an hour of glory. Where others would have been broken, ruined, and disgraced by the cross, Jesus saw it as the hour of his glory, saying "I, if I be lifted up from the earth, I'll draw all (persons) unto me" (John 12:32, KJV). God's own anointed being glorified by being crucified? What a strange glory!

Yes, "in many and various ways God spoke of old to our fathers by the prophets; but in these last days he has spoken to us by a Son. . . . " The Old Testament recorded great manifestations of God's glory in fire and brightness, in clouds and smoke, in mountains that quaked, in temples whose foundations shook, and in the visions of the prophets. But the New Testament reminds us that the greatest manifestation of God's glory was in a human life having been appointed heir of all things, through whom the world was created, who reflects the glory of God, and bears the very stamp of God's nature.

The heavens declare the glory of God and the firmament shows forth God's handiwork. Every time dawn comes to chase away the shadows of night, God is glorified. Every time the stars come out to light the midnight sky, God is glorified. Every time a rainbow appears after the storm, God is glorified. Every time a grain of wheat falls into the ground and dies, but rises with a new body, God is glorified. But God is glorified most when God is glorified in a human life.

That's why in the latter days God spoke to us through a son. It has been said that when the angels heard about Christ's mission of redemption they asked him: "Shall ten thousand of us weave our wings together to make a chariot for you to ride upon in your descent to that fallen people?" But Christ said, "No!" The angels then exclaimed, "Shall we bring together all the clouds of heaven and make a suitable throne for you to be seated on?" Again Christ's answer was "No!" The angels asked, "Shall we form an entourage of ten thousand legions to escort you to earth?" And yet again Christ said "No!" But travelling through the corridors of time, he stepped across forty-two generations until he was born in human flesh. The amazed angelic host which crowded on heaven's balcony to see him descend became excited and talked so loudly about the love of God for humanity that the shepherds in Bethlehem's fields heard them shouting, "Glory to God in the highest."[1]

It may seem strange when we think about how God can get the glory out of our wretched lives, but its not strange. *It's not strange!* It's the wonderful work of salvation, grace, love, and forgiveness accomplished by Jesus.

John said,

> Behold, what manner of love the Father has bestowed upon us, that we should be called God's children . . . Beloved, now are we God's children and it doth not yet appear what we shall be, but we know that, when he shall appear, we shall be like him; for we shall see him as he is" (1 John 3:1, 2).

In spite of ourselves, God can still get the glory out of our lives. Despite the devil's tricks and sin's snare, God can still get the glory out of our lives. Though we leave undone what we ought to have done, and do what we ought not to do, God can still get the glory out of our lives. In his song "My Tribute" Andrae Crouch said:

> How can I say thanks for the things you have done for me,
> Things so undeserved, yet you give to prove your love to me;

The voices of a million angels could not express my gratitude.
All that I am or ever hope to be, I owe it all to Thee.[1]
To God be the glory, To God be the glory,
To God be the glory, For the things He had done.
With His blood He has saved me, With His power He has raised
me.
To God be the glory, For the things he has done.[2]
Just let me live my life, Let it be pleasing Lord to Thee,
And should I gain any praise, Let it go to Calvary.
With His blood He has saved me, With His power He has raised
me,
To God be the glory for the things He has done.

The Manger-Maker

Luke 2:7

The sun was setting over ancient Palestine, as it had done so many times before, when the wife of the manger-maker walked to the door of the little workshop in the back of the house, as she had done so many times before, to tell her husband that the evening meal was ready. Occasionally she would pause, as she was then doing, to observe her husband deeply engrossed in his work.

As she watched him moving around amidst the evening shadows of the setting sun, she took note of his full beard and head of hair which seemed to turn more grey with each passing day. When he raised his hammer and brought it down accurately and forcefully upon its intended object, she noticed the large veins protruding from his arms and neck, and the muscles in his strong arms which had been preserved by years of physical work and conditioning.

She could remember when his hair had been as red as the rays of the setting sun, which was casting its final light for that day upon the earth and was bathing the little workshop in an amber glow. She could remember when the veins were not so prominent in his hands and the muscle tone in his arms was even more sleek. How she loved this man! Theirs had been a good marriage and the years had gone by quickly.

The wife allowed herself the luxury of remembering when

she had been a fair damsel and had been attracted to this young lad, whom she had met one day as she accompanied her mother to the village well. She had seen him there with his mother. His finger was bleeding. Someone had left a broken water pitcher by the well and he had tried to rearrange the pieces together. He had cut himself with one of the jagged edges of the broken pottery.

For as long as she had known him, he had loved to fix things and work with his hands. What had started out as curiosity about things that could be carved from wood or made with stone had turned into a skill and then into a career. The manger-maker had become a master craftsman and had become known throughout the region for the quality of his work. He believed that his work represented him, so he always tried to do it well. He was never out of work because his customers always came back. There were others who could do faster work and possibly fancier work but no one could do any better work. In addition to the constant work from old customers, there were always new customers who had heard of the old manger-maker's skill and would come from near and far with work to be done.

As his wife observed him and reflected on their life together, he looked up with a twinkle in his eyes. The twinkle was always there when he looked at her, even after all these years. He asked, "Is it suppertime already?" "Yes," she replied, "time to wash up and come to eat. By the way, what are you working on so intently? Anything special?"

"No," he said, "just another manger. Reuben, who owns an inn down in Bethlehem, needs another manger. This new decree from Caesar Augustus, requiring everyone to return to their hometown to register for the census, has brought an unusual amount of business to Bethlehem and to Reuben's inn this year. He was telling me that he stays full just about all of the time. He needs another manger for his guests' animals. This is no special project; it's just another manger."

The old workman soon finished the manger and inspected it, confident that he had done his usual quality job. This was far from being the first manger he had made and hopefully it would not be his last. Since he put his best effort into all of his work, this manger, from his perspective, was just another manger.

It wasn't necessary for the innkeeper who received the manger to inspect it too closely because he knew that the manger-maker didn't do shoddy work. The innkeeper knew that the insides would be hallowed out deep enough to hold sufficient hay and feed for the cattle and other animals who would eat from it. He knew that there would be no cracks in its bottom or sides which would allow water to seep in. He knew that the manger would be strong enough to take the kicks and scraping from the hooves of the animals who would use it. This was not the first manger that the innkeeper had ordered from the manger-maker and hopefully it would not be his last. So for the innkeeper it was just another manger.

Just another manger; that's probably what the maintenance men at the Bethlehem inn thought as they carried it to the stable in back of the inn and found a convenient place for the feeding of the animals.

Just another superstitious Hebrew; that's probably what Pharaoh thought when Moses first showed up at his court with the command that God's people be set free. *Just another meddlesome woman who has gotten out of her place;* that's probably what Sisera and his generals thought when they first heard that the prophetess Deborah was giving courage to the armies of Israel. *Just another preacher trying to make trouble. We'll intimidate him and buy him off like we've done all the rest;* that's probably what Ahab and Jezebel thought of Elijah when he declared that the rains would come only at his word. *Just another Indian;* that's probably what the British thought when Mahatma Gandhi first told them to go home and leave India to the Indians. *Just another black preacher;* that's probably what white America first thought when Dr. Martin Luther King, Jr. became spokesman for the Montgomery bus boycott. *Just another Black African;* that's probably what the white South African government first thought of Bishop Desmond Tutu when he began to challenge apartheid.

We must be careful about how we dismiss and take lightly those who have been made by the Master Crafter. Never sell yourself short. Never dismiss yourself as being a nobody with nothing special to offer. Recognize the fact that you have been made by the Master Crafter.

Others may treat us as just another employee, another student, another black or woman, but we are the work of the Master Crafter. We are "a chosen generation, a royal priesthood, a holy nation, a peculiar people" (1 Peter 1:9, KJV). Though we may look ordinary, God has suited us in our ordinariness for the purposes that we are to serve. Our insides have been hollowed out so that they can hold hearts to love God, minds to serve God, spirits that long for God, and souls to live eternally with God. God has given us the blood of Jesus to seal the cracks in our lives so that no sin can seep in to destroy what we are within. We are strengthened by God to withstand the kicks and bruises that others—Satan and life itself—give to us. We are the work of the Master Crafter.

Making mangers was not a particularly noteworthy calling. However, it was the manger-maker's calling and so he did his best. He didn't allow others to belittle his talents. He was proud of his work so he did his best.

No matter how many or how few, how great or how small your talents, if they are your talents, always put forth your best effort. No matter how great or how small your contribution when it is your time to give, give with thanksgiving, with pride, and with style. No matter how great or small the occasion when it is your time to perform, give it your all. We have no need to be jealous of another's task or talent, gift or role. All we have to do is strive for excellence in that which is ours to do.

The manger-maker had no way of knowing the special use to which his manger would be put. Thank God that he was consistent at producing his best. Thank God that the manger into which the baby Jesus was lain was among the manger-maker's best efforts. Heaven forbid that our Lord would have lain in a manger that proved insufficient for its unexpected blessing.

Heaven forbid that Jesus, who was born in the meanest, poorest, and crudest of circumstances, would have been laid in a manger of shoddy materials and poor workmanship.

We ought to always put forth our best effort because we never know when God will have some special use for our talent, our witness or testimony, or our life. We never know when we will be needed to fill a specific place, serve a special role, or be a unique part of God's larger plan of redemption. We ought to always put forth our best effort for we never know when God will visit our lives.

Thank God that Abraham was consistently courteous to strangers. On that day when he saw two strangers approaching his tent, he received them with his usual courtesy. He didn't realize it, but those two ordinary-looking men were angels on their way to Sodom and Gomorrah to deliver God's word of judgment. Because Abraham extended his best self, he received the assurance that God's word would still come true. His wife, Sarah, though far beyond childbearing years, would still give him a son, and Abraham would be the father of a great nation.

It always pays to put forth our best because we never know when heaven will descend upon our lives in search of our best. That's why Jesus told the disciples: "Watch therefore, for you do not know on what day the Lord is coming" (Matthew 24:42).

On the night that Jesus was born, a manger had a place in the drama of salvation. Who would have thought that at this particular time and place in history the God of the universe would have used something as insignificant as a manger? Who would have thought that at such an important point in time, on such a momentous occasion as the coming of the long-awaited Messiah, that something as simple and as small as a manger would have had such a prominent role?

One could conceive of God using the forces of nature. God had used rain in the time of Noah and fire in the time of Moses. During the Egyptian bondage God used all kinds of natural plagues to free the children of Israel. God sent the whirlwind for Elijah and God would use the stars to guide the wise men to the baby Jesus. Throughout the Scriptures the mighty forces of nature are used to accomplish God's will, but who would have thought that God would have needed and used something as small and as simple, but as important in that place and at that time, as a mere manger?

One would expect the involvement of human beings in the drama of salvation. One would expect prophets to foretell of a coming Messiah. In the event of a child's birth, one would expect the involvement of human parents. One would not even be surprised to learn of holy people like Simeon and Anna celebrating the Messiah's coming. One could conceive of visitors, even shepherds, coming to see him. When one considers that Jesus comes to challenge and rebuke the hold of Satan and sin on human life and destiny, one is not surprised to find an evil Herod plotting to destroy him. But who would have expected God to have needed and used something as simple and as small, but yet as important in that place and in that time, as a mere manger?

One is not surprised to see the involvement of angels. After all, throughout the Scriptures angels are associated with God's special communication with us. Since God used angels when he spoke in various ways in times past to our mothers and fathers, it would be expected that angels would be involved when God was communicating with us through a Son whom he had appointed heir of all things and through whom God also created the world. With the coming of God in Jesus one would expect to hear angels singing "Glory to God in the highest, and on earth peace among men and [women] with whom God is well pleased" (Luke 2:14). Angels and the baby Jesus just naturally go together. However, what one would not expect is the involvement of something as simple and as small but yet as important, at that time and in that place, as a manger, in this, the greatest story ever told.

However, at that time and in that place, nothing but a manger would do because the baby Jesus needed some place to lay his head. Mary and Joseph and the others would not have been able to hold him all of the time. The baby Jesus would have been constantly shifted from person to person. The ground would have been too hard and cold for him. The forces of nature—fire, wind, and rain—would not have been able to cushion the head of Jesus. Angels' music, while sweet, was not designed to be a resting place for a baby's head. Since cribs are not found in stables, the only thing that could serve that purpose was something as simple as the feeding trough of the stable animals—the manger.

If God can use something as simple and as small as a manger, then God can use you and me. We may not be able to sing like angels and we may not be able to preach like Paul, but if God can use something as simple and small as the manger, God can use you and me. There may be others better qualified, with more energy and strength, with more money and influence, but if God is big enough to use something small like the manger of a good craftsman, since we have been made by the Master Crafter, God can use you and me.

As unbelievable as it may seem, maybe what God needs in a particular situation, to reach a particular person, is not somebody else but you or me. Maybe somebody needs to hear us tell our story—as only we can—of how Jesus lifted us from sinking sand. Maybe somebody who "knew us when" needs to see the change that Jesus has made in our lives. Every now and then we can be God's mangers—serving a special purpose in special situations at special times.

It was just another manger; that's probably what everyone thought as they dealt with the manger in which Jesus was laid. How could they possibly know that the God of the universe had a special purpose for that manger? How could they know that something far more precious than fodder for cattle or feed for animals would lay in that manger? How could they know that that manger would be the first resting place for God's unspeakable gift? How could they know that the angels would sing over that manger? How could they know that that manger, which looked so ordinary, would be unlike any other manger that had ever been made? How could they know that such an ordinary manger would hold such an extraordinary treasure? How could they know that after two thousand years we are still talking about, singing about, and preaching about that manger? Manger! Manger! Manger!

Away in a manger, no crib for a bed,
the little Lord Jesus laid down his sweet head.
The stars in the bright sky looked down where he lay,
the little Lord Jesus, asleep on the hay.

No Room

Luke 2:7

Like an arrow which pierces the heart or a clap of thunder which startles, so do the words of our text grip the sensitivities of the believing Christian. There is a kind of pathos which surrounds the words of our text as we think about our Lord and Saviour being born in a stable because there was no room in the inn to receive him. No room to receive Jesus and so he is pushed to the outer periphery to be born.

The context, circumstances, and characters differ, but the malady of overcrowded and unconcerned lives remains even to this day. It is easy to accuse the innkeeper of all kinds of gross negligence and put the total responsibility upon him for the mean circumstances in which Jesus was born. It is easy to debate whether or not the innkeeper did all that he possibly could to provide Mary and Joseph with lodging within the inn. Jesus, however, faces the same problem today—no room.

Maybe one of the reasons we are inclined to come down hard on the Bethlehem innkeeper is because we feel guilty about doing the same thing to Jesus—not leaving sufficient room in our hearts and lives to wholly receive him when he comes.

Some of the people whom we dislike the most, we dislike because they are just like us, not because they are different from us. Both good qualities and faults that we so readily see in

32

others, we easily overlook in ourselves. Often what we dislike about other people is the potential we recognize in ourselves for behaving in the same manner that they do. Consequently, whenever we look at the Bethlehem innkeeper we ought also to look at ourselves.

It should be observed that the innkeeper displayed no hostility toward the first family of the new dispensation. It cannot be proven that he withheld any extra rooms from them; the account simply tells us that he just didn't have any room. There was no room because others had arrived before Joseph and Mary. If they had arrived earlier, they no doubt would have been accommodated, however earlier arrivals had taken up all of the space.

The time of our text was a particularly busy one for the Bethlehem innkeeper. The census taken during the reign of Caesar Augustus, which required everyone to enroll themselves in the town of their birth, had brought a great influx of persons to Bethlehem, thus straining all of the private and public facilities of the town. Bethlehem, far from being a major population center like Jerusalem, was a relatively small and insignificant town. The prophet Micah informs us of this in his prophecy that Bethlehem would be the home of the promised Messiah. Centuries before Christ's birth Micah had declared:

> But you, O Bethlehem Ephrathah,
>   who are little among the
>   clans of Judah,
> from you shall come forth for me
>   one who is to be ruler in Israel,
> whose origin is from of old,
>   from ancient days.
>   —Micah 5:2

Although the innkeeper probably felt gratified for the increased business that the census was bringing to town, he must have also been frustrated because he really had more business than he could handle. His facility was built to accommodate only so many persons. With his inn being so overcrowded and with so many requests and demands, he could give some attention to everybody but he didn't have time to give anybody the kind of specialized attention that they deserved or that he might have desired.

It's good to be busy and productive, but sometimes our lives can be overcrowded to the point that we don't do much of anything well. There are times in which we are exceptionally busy, in which we may fall behind and must run to catch up. But some of our lives are so crowded with commitments that we run all of the time. Somebody told us that busyness was the sign of a productive life, so from the time we rise to the time we lay down, we are rushing and trying to get a lot done and worrying about how we are going to do it all. When we stop to think about it, much of what we worry about doing and most of what we run ourselves down trying to do really isn't that important.

A friend of mine once remarked to me that she didn't how how she was going to get everything done which she had to do that very day. I said to her, "Do you know what will happen if you don't do it all?" She said, "What?" I said, "Well, tomorrow morning the sun will rise as usual, the earth will continue to turn, people will continue to go about their business as usual, and you will wake up and discover that neither the world at large or your own world fell apart because you went to bed with some things left undone that you believed had to be done."

One of the hard realities that some of us need to face is the truth that we cannot do everything we want to do without something being crowded out. When we are trying to hold down a full-time job or career, a full time marriage and/or a relationship, full-time child-rearing, time-consuming and energy-draining church, civic, and social involvements, something or somebody is going to be crowded out. We don't have enough room physically, mentally, or emotionally for everything and everybody that we allow to make claims upon our lives. We are only built to accommodate so much. Better to do a few things well than a lot of things sloppily. At some point we really need to decide what is necessary and what is an optional, what really must be done and what we simply would like to do. Otherwise we will find ourselves neglecting what we should not neglect and giving our time and attention to what we really could neglect.

Many times, as our text demonstrates, when life gets over-crowded, Jesus is often pushed out. The church and Jesus, not social commitments or some spur of the moment item we bought, are considered to be the expendable items on too many of our overcrowded dockets. When money gets tight, for many of us, our church commitments become expendable.

A member once came to me and said, "Rev., my wife and I just moved into our new house and we have to cut back in our giving to the church. I hope you will understand." My reply was, "Instead of cutting back on your stewardship to the One who made it possible for you to move into that new house, why don't you cut back on some of your social activities?"

Some of us don't intend to crowd the Savior out; other things have simply gotten a hold on our lives. Our lives have a number of earlier arrivals—sins which give us pleasure, habits that we support and maintain, routines that we have established (we do certain things with certain people at certain times), grudges that we nurse, bad feelings that we cling to—and we can't let anything interfere with them. Consequently we have no room—no energy, no time, no money—left for Jesus.

There were guests at the inn who, no doubt, saw Mary's condition, but none of the early arrivals were willing to give up their places. Wrong never willingly steps aside for right. Habits never willingly step aside for change. Satan never willingly relinquishes his place to the Holy Spirit. Once routine has been established, once sin has gotten a foothold, they don't offer to give up their places to make room for Jesus. The only way a place can be made is by the Keeper of Life making a decision to find some room.

As I think about the birth of our Lord in a stable, I believe that if the innkeeper had known who it was who was looking for lodging, he would have found some room in his inn. If he had known the great opportunity and great honor that stood upon his threshold when Joseph and Mary came seeking a night's lodging, I believe he would have made room. If he had known that his inn had been chosen as the birthplace of the world's Saviour, I'm sure he would have made room. If he had known that the woman who stood before him bore in her bosom Solomon's Rose of Sharon and Daniel's Ancient of Days, I'm sure he would have found room. If he had known that Mary bore the One whom the prophets said would be called Emmanuel, meaning "God with us," I'm sure he would have found room. But the last thing that was on the innkeeper's mind that night as he ran to and fro dealing with his overcrowded inn was the promised Messiah.

The irony of Jesus' birth was that he was looked for, hoped for, and prayed for, but wasn't expected when he came. All the innkeeper saw before him was a tired, dusty male with a tired, dusty, pregnant woman riding a tired, dusty donkey. So he sent them to his dusty stable and continued looking after his overcrowded inn. But while the innkeeper did business as usual, God did the unusual and brought forth a child, born of a virgin, whose name was called Jesus because he would save God's people from their sins.

Although the birth took place on his property, the innkeeper didn't even know what was happening in his own backyard. He wasn't alerted to the Christ event that was taking place right under his nose. Shepherds on the other side of town, who were watching their flocks by night, were told of the Savior's birth and were invited to the celebration. Wise men in a distant land read the message of a newborn king in a star and were moved to search for Jesus until they found him. But the innkeeper in whose stable all of this was happening was not even invited to the celebration. It wasn't that the innkeeper was being snubbed, heaven simply reasoned that anybody who was too busy to make room for Jesus' birth in his inn, would also be too busy to come to his party and celebrate his coming into the world.

Let us never allow our hearts and lives to become so

crowded that we fail to be part of what God may be doing right in our midst, right under our noses, right in our backyards, right in our church. God's Spirit may be pouring out blessings all around us but, because our lives are so crowded with trivialities, game playing, turf guarding, and petty politics; because our hearts are so full of hell and our minds are so full of venom, we don't have room to receive Jesus who wants to be born in our lives.

It's dangerous when we allow our hearts and lives to become too crowded with the things and cares of this world, for the word of the Scripture is clear: If we have not found room enough in our hearts and lives for Jesus to be born, then we will not be part of the celebration when he comes back again with the power of the ages in his hands and the glory of the heavens wrapped around his shoulders to claim a church without spot or blemish. If we have been too busy to answer when he came knocking on the door of our lives, then we will not be invited to the party when he comes again, when those who have allowed him to be born in their lives are caught up to meet him and are changed from mortality to immortality in the twinkling of an eye.

Jesus has promised that if we make room for him, then he will make room for us. He told his disciples one day: "I'm going away and you're going to have some difficult days ahead of you. But, 'let not your hearts be troubled; believe in God, believe also in me. In my Father's house are many rooms, if it were not so I would have told you. I go to prepare a place for you. And if I go and prepare a place for you, I will come again, and receive you unto myself; that where I am, there you may be also' " (John 14:1-3).

Why Were the Wise Men Wise?

Matthew 2:1

When Jesus was born in Bethlehem of Judaea in the days of Herod the king, wise men from the East came to Jerusalem seeking him and inquiring, "Where is he who has been born king of the Jews? For we have seen his star in the East, and have come to worship him."

Who were these wise men, from whence did they come, and whither did they go? Other than their brief appearance in Matthew's Gospel, we do not hear anymore about them in Scripture.

Frankly, we do not know exactly who they were, where they came from or what happened to them. Although we can't answer these questions with historical preciseness and accuracy, much research has been done on them and many legends and traditions have been developed about them.

According to some, they were kings; according to some, they were priests; according to some, they were scientists or astrologers; while still others claimed they were sorcerers or magicians. My own research indicates that the "Magi," a term which we translate as wise men, were descendants of an ancient tribe of people known as Medes who were part of the old Persian Empire. At one time the Medes had aspirations of overthrowing the Persians and establishing their own empire. However, they had long given up their ambitions for power and prestige and had become an order or tribe of priests. They were, in Persia, what the Levites were in Israel. Like Daniel and to a certain extent Joseph, the Magi were regarded as men of holiness and wisdom who advised and instructed kings. As learned holy men, they interpreted dreams and offered sacrifices to God. As teacher-priests they were skilled in medicine and the sciences, as well as philosophy.

In their quest for the truth, the wise men studied the stars. They knew that the stars never varied in their courses as they made their way across the heavens. The same pattern that the stars follow now is the pattern that Adam and Eve observed when they looked up at their first starlit sky in Paradise.

For the wise men, the stars represented the unbroken order of the universe. They believed that a person's destiny was governed by the star under which he or she was born. Thus, if the unvarying order of the heavens was disturbed by the sudden appearance of some unusually bright star, they would naturally conclude that God was breaking through creation and order and announcing something special.

We do not know what star the wise men saw. We just know that as they watched the starlit heavens, some peculiar heavenly brilliance spoke to them about the entry of a special person, a king, into the world. This king was so special that he had his own star. None of the kings that they had known had their own star. Not Darius, or Cyrus, or Nebuchadnezzar, not any of the Egyptian Pharaohs, nor any of the Roman Caesars, not even David or Solomon or any of Israel's other kings had their own stars. In the midst of heaven's unbroken pattern of stars that had been the same since the dawning of time, a new star appeared to announce the arrival of a new king. In their search of the ancient scriptures, they were led to Palestine.

When Jesus was born in Bethlehem of Judaea in the days of Herod the king, wise men from the east came to Jerusalem saying, "Where is he who has been born king of the Jews? For we have seen his star in the East, and have come to worship him."

Why were these wise men so wise? Based upon the number of gifts presented to the Christ child, tradition has established the number of the wise men who came seeking the newborn king to be three. Now there were many, many more than three wise men in the ancient world. Something as prominent as a new bright star in the heavens could not be hidden. Other wise men of that time who customarily studied the heavens also, undoubtedly, saw this star. The star which the wise men saw in the East may have even been visible to those who lived in Palestine.

I don't know how Palestinian wise men missed it, unless they had simply failed to look up. Maybe they were so busy contending with things around them that they forgot to look up. Maybe they were so busy complaining about Caesar, watching their backs for the next trick from Herod, plotting against Pilate, or working on each other, that they failed to look up and see the same star in the same heavens that the wise men saw in the East.

No matter what happens around us or to us, it pays to look up sometimes. I once saw an old hog standing under an oak tree gobbling up all the acorns that he saw on the ground. While he was eating acorns, others occasionally fell out of the tree and several even fell on him, but the hog never stopped his activity. Because the hog had his head down and wasn't watching where he was going, he bumped into the tree several times, but he never stopped eating. With all of that moving around and eating, not once did the hog lift his head and look up to see where the acorns were coming from.

Every now and then it pays to pause from that which occupies our constant attention and look up. When we don't look up, we fail to see where our blessings are coming from. When we don't look up, we fail to see where our strength is coming from. That's why David said, "I will lift up my eyes unto the hill from whence comes my help. My help comes from the Lord who made the heavens and the earth" (Psalm 121:1-2, KJV). When we don't look up, we fail to see the warnings, comfort, and deliverance that God is sending to us. When we don't look up, we fail to receive the word about a Saviour who has come to give us even more of the blessings of life.

I don't know why the learned scribes and priestly Levites of Palestine did not see the star. I do not know why other wise men of the East, who also studied the skies and had access to the same scriptures, did not come with those who journeyed to Palestine. Maybe the others were too busy to take the time to go on such a long journey. Maybe some did not feel like going on such a long journey. Maybe others didn't attach as much significance or the same interpretation as those who came to Jerusalem.

All we know is that among those who either did see or could have seen the star announcing the birth of Jesus in Bethlehem of Judaea in the days of Herod the king, only three wise men came from the East saying, "Where is he who has been born king of the Jews? For we have seen his star in the East, and have come to worship him."

These wise men were wise enough to follow the star. God had sent a message from heaven and they were wise enough to take it seriously and to pack their necessary traveling gear, and go forth on a long journey to follow the star.

Wise people always follow where God leads them. Sometimes they don't know exactly where the journey will take them or how far it will take them from the hearths of homes and the warm embraces of family and friends whom they love. All they know is that they've seen a star in the heavens, they hear God calling them, they feel Christ beckoning them, and the Spirit pulling them. They can't be at peace until they follow their star. They don't know how long it will take them to reach the goal of their quest or just what they will find at its end, but they know they have received a message from heaven and they must follow their star.

Like the Israelites who left Egypt in search of Canaan and were guided by God's pillar of cloud by day and protected by God's pillar of fire by night, like the wise men who left the East to journey West following a star, so black people and others know what it is to leave the Egypt of the Southland and other places of oppression and follow stars of opportunity and freedom.

Harriet Tubman made over one hundred trips back into the South to lead black slaves to freedom. They travelled at night through woods and swamps, ofttimes without map or compass. She knew how to look up and be guided by the stars. She found her way and led others to freedom.

Frederick Douglass, who also ran away from slavery to freedom, remembered how important the stars were for black people traveling in the night; he named his newspaper the "North Star."

Thank God for the stars which are sent to guide those of us who follow where we are led. Some of us made the journey from south to north ourselves, and some of us didn't but we praise God for parents, grandparents, brothers and sisters, uncles and aunts, cousins and friends, who saw their stars shining in the heavens. They didn't know exactly what they were going to find up north but they saw a star pointing to freedom and a better life—they followed their star.

Sometimes we receive discouragement from those from whom we expected encouragement. Sometimes people don't see what we saw and because they didn't see or didn't understand what we saw, they try to discourage us. Sometimes others are afraid for us or hurt because they feel we don't appreciate the sacrifices they have made as they tried, as best they could, to provide for us. Some laugh at us and tell us we are going to fail. Some, with whom we have planned to make the journey, change their minds, and we have to go on by ourselves.

It isn't easy saying good-bye, but when we see our star we have to follow it. Wise people always follow their stars. Wise people always heed the messages God sends and follow where God leads. That's why I always tell people that if God has shown you a star, if God has given you a vision, if God has sent you a dream, then no matter who doesn't understand, follow your star. Even if you have to travel alone, follow your star. For wise people always follow their stars. It isn't the light that we see but the light that we follow which makes us wise.

When Jesus was born in Bethlehem of Judaea in the days of

Herod the king, there came wise men from the East saying, "Where is he who has been born king of the Jews, for we have seen his star in the East and have come to worship him." Among the many stars that shined in the heavens, there was only one that led to Jesus. The wise men were wise not simply because they saw the stars but because they followed the star that led to Jesus. Wise people always follow the star that leads to Jesus.

If there is one question that some of us need to ask ourselves, it is "Where is the star leading us?" If it is leading us away from God, then we are following the wrong star. If it is leading us away from the church, then we are following the wrong star. No matter how much money or prestige or power is at the end of our quest, no matter what position or office is at the end of our search, if the process that we use to reach it and the road that we take to get there leads us away from Jesus, then we are following the wrong star.

If the star we are following leads us to say things we shouldn't or do things we know are wrong, that if we were discovered we would be disgraced and ashamed, then we are following the wrong star. If the star that we are following causes us to forget the training received from praying mothers, believing fathers, and others who truly love us, then we are following the wrong star. If all there is at the end of our search is a cold grave and no hope of an eternal life in an eternal day, then we are following the wrong star.

But if the star that we are following leads to the One who is the Bright and Morning Star, if the days of our travel lead to One who is the Ancient of Days, if the nights of our quest lead to One who is the star of hope borne on the nocturnal bosom of the night, then we are following the right star. There is only one star that leads to Jesus. There is only one way—it is the knee way of prayer and confession; it is the way of repentance and the new birth; it is the way of the cross that leads to the victory of the empty tomb. And wise people always follow the star that leads to Jesus.

When the wise men found Jesus, they presented him with

gifts of gold, frankincense, and myrrh. Where did the wise men get these gifts? I doubt if the Jerusalem shopping mall would have been open for them to pick up something on their way to Bethlehem. They had to have brought their gifts from home, which meant that they were prepared to meet the newborn King. They didn't know how long or how far they would travel, or when or where the star would finally come to rest. Therefore, they were prepared to meet Jesus, the newborn King, whenever, wherever, and however they found him. The wise men were wise not only because they followed the star that led to Jesus, but they were wise because they were prepared to meet Jesus when they found him. Wise people always make preparations to meet Jesus. It makes no sense to come all the way to the end of our journey without having made preparations to meet Jesus.

What kind of preparations are we making to meet Jesus? What are we carrying along with us on our journey? Is what we are carrying in our hearts suitable to be laid before the King of kings?

Why follow the star that leads to the King, travel the King's highway and then come before the King unprepared? As your journey to the King nears its end, don't count on being able to run into some church to pick up some suitable gifts and graces for the King. Whatever has been in our hearts and whatever our lives have been all along on our journey is what we are going to have to give him. If we've been carrying excuses, that's all we can give. If we've been gossips, that's all we can give. If we've been carrying pettiness, that's all we can give.

Like the wise men, I want to be able to give suitable gifts to the King of my life. I hope to be able to give him the gold of a life that has been tested by the fires of trial so that the best has come forth. I want to give to him the kind of gold that Job spoke of when he said, "[My God] knows the way I take, and when He shall have tried me, I shall come forth like gold" (Job 23:10). I want to be able to give the frankincense of a life of service—I mean the kind of service that Isaiah committed himself to in the temple when he heard a voice say, "Who will go for us? Whom shall we send?" Isaiah answered, "Here am I, send me" (Isaiah 6:8). I want to be able to present him with the myrrh of a life of sacrifice; one that has died to an old life and been raised to a new one. I'm talking about the kind of death and resurrection that Paul spoke of when he said, "Whatever gain I had I counted it as loss for Christ's sake . . . that I might know him and the power of his resurrection" (Philippians 3:7, 10).

The wise men were wise because they followed their star. They were wise because they followed the star that led to Jesus. They were wise because they were prepared to meet Jesus. How wise are we? How wise are you?

Going Beyond Palm Sunday

John 12:12-19

It was Passover time and Jews had come from the ends of the earth to Jerusalem. Wherever Jews lived, it was their ambition to observe at least one Passover in Jerusalem. In addition to those who had come from afar, there were Jews who had come from within Palestine itself. The law required every adult male Jew who lived within twenty miles of Jerusalem to come to that holy city.

On one occasion a census was taken of the number of lambs slain at the Passover feast and the number was given at 265,000. A minimum of ten persons was required for each lamb. If this estimate is correct, then there must have been approximately 2,700,000 people at the Passover feast. Even if the numbers are exaggerated, the crowds must have been enormous and Jerusalem and all of its surrounding vicinity must have been packed with people.

At Passover time Jews remembered the deliverance of their ancestors from Egyptian bondage. Nationalistic feelings ran high during the time of Jesus, as the present generation of Israelites chafed under the yoke of Roman oppression. During Passover messianic hope and expectations were strongest. During Passover the Sadducees and the Roman guard, who were most concerned about keeping order, were always edgy lest some incident occur which might arouse the smouldering hostility and desire for freedom which were always just below the surface of an uneasy peace, awaiting the right moment to burst forth.

According to John's account, it was during Passover that Jesus had come to nearby Bethany to see about his good friend Lazarus. Jesus had raised Lazarus from the dead and news about this great miracle had reached Jerusalem, with its curious, restless, and hopeful crowds. Thus, as Jesus headed towards Jerusalem he was accompanied by an enthusiastic crowd that had been with him in Bethany and had seen his mighty work. Word went ahead that Jesus, the person who had raised Lazarus from the dead, was coming to town. A crowd of Passover pilgrims, some of whom were curious, some of whom were well wishers, and some of whom were the devout and who lived in constant readiness to receive the Messiah, went to greet Jesus and his followers. When the joyful Bethany crowd met with the expectant Jerusalem crowd amid the celebrative atmosphere of the Passover around them, a spontaneous combustion of excitement and spirit broke out.

Jesus, who was riding a donkey, was received like a conquering king. Some cut palm branches from the trees and waved them in the air and spread them along the road. Others spread their garments on the road. The multitudes shouted, "Hosanna to the Son of David! Blessed is he who comes in the name of the Lord, even the King of Israel!" Matthew's Gospel tells us that when Jesus entered Jerusalem there was so much rejoicing that the whole city was moved. John tells us that the Pharisees expressed dismay, remarking that the whole world had gone after him.

This had to have been a very significant day for the disciples who had left all to follow Jesus, for his friends who loved him, and for our Lord. If the writers of the Gospels had put down their pens and ended their accounts with Palm Sunday's triumphal entry, we would have had a nice, neatly packaged, essentially trouble-free success story.

What better place for the Gospels to end than at the moment when Jesus, the small town carpenter-turned-teacher and miracle-working prophet from Nazareth, rode in triumph to the praises of the multitudes as he entered big-time Jerusalem? What better place to end the Gospel story than at that moment when Jesus is riding the crest of popularity, acceptability, respectability, and success? What better place to end the Gospels than at that moment when the world seems to be literally falling at Jesus' feet and his future looks brighter than ever?

Yet we know that if the Gospels ended with the Palm Sunday event, they would be incomplete Gospels. If the Gospels ended with Palm Sunday, we might think that Palm Sunday was Jesus' greatest hour. If the Gospels ended with Palm Sunday, we might think that our Lord's message, ministry, and mission had truly been accepted and understood by those who cheered him. We might think that the crowds who greeted him stayed with him.

It's easy to be part of the Palm Sunday crowd. Everybody likes a winner; everybody likes to ride in on the coattails or be on the team of somebody who seems to be going places. When the multitudes are singing Jesus' praises, when following him is the "in" thing to do, when there are no risks, no inconveniences, no sacrifices, and no demands being placed upon our obedience, time, or talent; when no requests are being made for our money, it's easy to proclaim "Hosanna."

It's easy to join with Jesus in high moments of rapture and celebration. We naively wish that all moments will be like that one. But the Palm Sunday story, while gratifying, does not tell the whole story. Christians who walk with Jesus only on Palm Sunday, when things are going well and everybody seems happy, miss out on the real victory. Christians who see Jesus only as a conquering king living up to their own expectations miss out on the real message, ministry, and meaning of Jesus. People who don't go beyond a Palm Sunday mentality miss out on the essence of the Gospel.

To really understand who Jesus was, what he was about, and what he can really do for you, to you, in you, with you, and through you, you must go beyond Palm Sunday. Palm Sunday marks the beginning of Jesus' last week of earthly ministry before his death. And yet so much of what we know as the Gospel revolves around this last week.

In Matthew's Gospel the Palm Sunday story is found in chapter 21, but his Gospel doesn't end until chapter 28. In Mark's work, the Palm Sunday event appears in chapter 11 but his work does not end until chapter 16. About one-third of Matthew's and Mark's Gospels are devoted to what happened after Palm Sunday. In the Gospel of Luke, Palm Sunday is found in chapter 19, but his Gospel does not end until chapter 24. About one-fourth of Luke's Gospel tells about what happened to Jesus after Palm Sunday. In John's Gospel Palm Sunday occurs in chapter 12, but his Gospel does not end until chapter 21. Almost one-half of John's Gospel would be left out if we stopped with Palm Sunday.

If we want to understand the Gospels fully, if we want to be the Christians that God would like us to be, we must go beyond Palm Sunday in our attitudes toward life. We must go beyond Palm Sunday in our thinking about religion. We must go beyond Palm Sunday in our devotion to Christ. We must go beyond Palm Sunday in our living unto God in the power of the Holy Spirit.

To attain the fullness of the knowledge of the Lord Jesus Christ, we must go beyond Palm Sunday. We must follow Jesus on that Monday after Palm Sunday when he went into the temple and saw merchants buying and selling, scheming and extorting, cheating and lying, and drove them out of his Father's house. If we are to grow beyond our Palm Sunday naivete, we must first come to grips with the imperfections of the church.

So many times seasoned as well as new Christians have become discouraged because we see so much of the same behavior and attitudes in the church as we see in the world. As in many of you, I wish that the church, as we know it, were perfect. But if it were, I couldn't belong and you couldn't belong. The church is not made up of perfect people but rather imperfect people who are striving for perfection. As in any struggle, sometimes we fail and sometimes we succeed, but we keep on striving just the same. And although our temples and our efforts are not perfect, we are still in God's house. And because we are in God's house, every now and then Jesus does come by. Whenever we stray too far away from where we ought to be, Jesus has a way of shaking us, awakening us, and bringing us back in line.

We must go beyond Palm Sunday and follow Jesus on the Tuesday after, when he debated with those who criticized him and tried to discredit his teachings. On Palm Sunday we become lost in the ecstasy of the crowd and believe that everybody appreciates what is going on. We must go beyond Palm Sunday to discover that righteousness has its foes.

Contrary to our observations, everybody wasn't rejoicing on Sunday. Everybody didn't appreciate our acts of praise. Some were jealous because of the attention we received on Palm Sunday. They question and challenge us, not to learn but to make us angry. They take away our joy and cause us to doubt ourselves and our faith.

But we can't allow a Tuesday devil to take our Palm Sunday spirit; we can't allow a Tuesday gossip to steal our Sunday joy; we can't allow a Tuesday busybody to deter us from the business of the kingdom. We can't lose our religion on—or over—a Tuesday critic. Like Jesus, all we can do is answer them with the power of God's Word and hold on to the profession of our own faith without wavering.

We must move beyond Palm Sunday and follow Jesus on the Wednesday after. On Wednesday Judas, one of Jesus' own chosen disciples, made contact with the authorities to betray the Lord. On Wednesday, according to Matthew and Mark, while Jesus was dining he received one of the last kindnesses of his earthly life. A woman, out of heartfelt love and gratitude, poured a flask of costly perfume upon Jesus lifting his spirit.

One of the painful lessons we learn when we go beyond Palm Sunday is that every church, every family, every circle of friends or associates has a Judas. Sometimes those who do us the greatest harm are not those from without but those from within. But for every Judas who betrays our trust, there is someone else who responds to our kindness with an act of love and thanksgiving. For every Judas who discourages us, there is someone else to lift our spirits. For every Judas who tears us down, there is somebody else to build us up. For every Judas who digs a ditch, there is somebody else who anoints us for greater service. For every Judas who hurts us, there is someone else to comfort.

We must move beyond Palm Sunday and follow Jesus to the Thursday after. Follow him to the upper room where Jesus sat down with the disciples at the Last Supper, broke bread, and said, "Take, eat; this is my body." Jesus took the cup and when he had given thanks he gave it to them saying, "Drink of it, all of you; for this is my blood of the covenant, which is poured out for many for the forgiveness of sins" (Matthew 26:27).

When you go beyond Palm Sunday, you will learn to say good-bye to those you love. When you go beyond Palm Sunday, you can make sacrifices for those you love even though present circumstances may indicate that your sacrifices are in vain.

Follow Jesus on Thursday into Gethsemane and hear his prayer: "My Father, if it be possible, let this cup pass from me; nevertheless, not as I will, but as thou wilt" (Matthew 26:39). When you go beyond Palm Sunday, you can pray your way through your darkest hour until you attain the victory which comes by faith. Follow Jesus on Thursday, as he stood before his accusers with power to destroy and never said a mumbling word. When you go beyond Palm Sunday you can face Satan's rage with a spirit of peace and calmness.

We must go beyond Palm Sunday and follow Jesus on Good Friday as he bore an old rugged cross up to Calvary's brow. For Jesus still says to us, "If anyone would come after me let them leave the security of the Palm Sunday crowd, deny themselves, and take up their cross and follow me." Follow Jesus to the tomb where the authorities hastily laid him to wait for another day to prepare his body for final burial. When you go beyond Palm Sunday you learn how to bury your pain in the face of heartbreaking Calvary experiences and wait upon God.

Somebody might ask, "Does the Gospel end here?" The answer to that question is an emphatic no! Matthew's Gospel records Jesus' crucifixion and burial in chapter 27, but there's another chapter. In Mark the crucifixion and burial are found in chapter 15, but there's another chapter. In Luke's Gospel the crucifixion and burial are found in chapter 23, but there's another chapter. In John the crucifixion and burial are found in chapter 19, but there are two more chapters.

Never forget that there's another chapter beyond Good Friday. There's another chapter beyond suffering and tribulation, heartache and pain, sickness and death. There's another chapter beyond Satan and sin. It's a chapter that tells the story of faithful women who went to the tomb to anoint a dead body but received a message from living angels about a living Lord whom Calvary could not destroy, death couldn't keep, and the grave couldn't hold. It's a chapter that tells about the real victory of Jesus.

When Jesus rode into Jerusalem on Palm Sunday, he dismounted from a donkey. But when Jesus arose on Easter, he arose to dismount no more. John on Patmos said: "I saw heaven opened, and beheld a white horse! He who sat upon it is called Faithful and True . . . On his robe and on his thigh he has a name inscribed, King of Kings and Lord of Lords" (Revelation 19:11).

The real victory was not seen by any great Palm Sunday multitudes, but by the faithful who walked with Jesus beyond Palm Sunday. If we would share in that real victory, then we too must move beyond Palm Sunday and witness with Jesus in the temple on Monday; defend Jesus on Tuesday; comfort Jesus on Wednesday; pray with Jesus on Thursday; bear a cross for Jesus on Friday; wait for Jesus on Saturday. Then we can shout victory on Sunday morning as we receive the news from the angel ". . . you seek Jesus who was crucified. He is not here; for he has risen! He has risen! Hallelujah, he has risen."

When Jesus Prays for Us

Luke 22:31-32

I've always been fascinated and amazed at the Lord's ability to recognize potential. No matter how ordinary or untalented a person seems to be, the Lord can always see the potential for greatness.

For years people saw Peter and John fishing in the sea of Galilee and thought nothing about it. They just assumed that Peter would never be anything other than an ordinary fisherman. But one day Jesus looked at him and said, "Peter you can be a fisher of people, a preacher, a pillar of the church. Simon, you can be a rock."

The Lord knew Peter better than Peter knew himself. The Lord knew that Peter was hotheaded and brash, that many times he spoke before he thought, that he could be easily influenced, that he cracked under pressure, and that Peter was not as courageous as he seemed to be.

But the Lord also knew that Peter was basically loyal and devoted, and that his heart and intentions were for the best; that he simply lacked the inner strength to stick to his guns. The Lord knew that in spite of his faults, Peter had the potential for being a great leader. And even though he irked the other disciples sometimes, Peter still commanded their respect. Maybe it was because the others recognized his sincerity or maybe it was because he was so outspoken. Many times when Peter spoke, he was probably expressing the doubts, misunderstandings, and anxieties that the other disciples felt but were too afraid to express. There was just something about Peter that made him emerge as a leader.

Jesus recognized all of this. But he wasn't the only one who saw Peter's potential for leadership and greatness—Satan recognized it also. Don't ever make the mistake of thinking that the Lord is the only one with an eye on us, Satan is watching also. As the Lord is pleased when we do good and do right, Satan is angered.

Many persons have discovered that, once they start attending church and try to live better lives, their troubles and problems increase. When we are neutral—not actively serving the Lord or the devil too much—then Satan is happy. We pose no threat to Satan's evil work in the world and there's no need for Satan to throw any roadblocks in our way. When we're actively serving Satan, Satan is not going to put any obstacle in our way. Satan wants to keep us happy, so Satan's going to let us have our wishes whether we need them or ought to have them. But when we are trying to get closer to the Lord, when we're trying to live a righteous life, Satan becomes uneasy. Satan sees us as potential adversaries and threats to the ongoing work of evil. Every child of God who knows the value of prayer is a threat to unrighteousness and evil.

A closer walk with the Lord means that Satan has one less mouth for gossip, one less mind to conjure up an evil design, one less set of hands to do evil bidding, one less pair of feet to trample on good people, one less life to use and misuse for Satan's own purposes.

When we line up with God we automatically line up against Satan. So Satan, in order to discourage us and weaken our faith and turn us around, will throw all kinds of hindrances and setbacks in our paths in an attempt to show us that serving God and trying to do right and live clean and honest lives doesn't pay. Satan will use anything and anybody. Satan will enter our workplace, where we've been doing well, and create problems there. Satan will come into our home and create tensions over money and bills between husband and wife, parent and child. Satan will come into the church and discourage us in the very place where we are building a spiritual foundation. Satan will use our enemies and, if that doesn't work, Satan will use those closest to us—our own family, our friends, sometimes even the minister or other leading members of the church—anyone in whom we have faith. Satan will put us through a living hell to break us.

Sometimes we ask why the Lord puts so much upon us. Well, many times it isn't the Lord piling burdens upon us, it's Satan. If we're serving God, why would God put trouble in our path or a cross on our back? After all, God didn't put Jesus on the cross, that was the work of sin and evil. God raised Jesus up after sin, evil and death had done all that they could.

If your cross is heavy, don't blame God—blame Satan. Jesus said, "My yoke is not grievous, my yoke is easy and my burdens are light" (Matthew 11:30). There's a joy in serving the Lord. If you don't have any joy in your religion, don't blame God—blame Satan, because Satan is the one who stole it from you. God is the one who gives us strength to withstand the assaults of the wicked and to bear the burdens that Satan seeks to impose.

Jesus knew that, in spite of Simon's faults, he was still a good person. In spite of his shortcomings, Peter could still become a great preacher and a great leader. Jesus also knew that Satan recognized Peter's potential. That's why, during the Last Supper, he turned suddenly to his good friend and said, "Simon, Simon, behold, Satan demanded to have you." He doesn't call him Peter, the Rock Man, but plain old "Simon."

All of us have the potential to crumble under the attack of the devil. We never become strong enough or run this race so well that we are immune to the attack of the devil. We never become so steadfast that the devil can't make us stumble. For at a time when we least expect it, in a meeting when we least expect it, from a person whom we least suspect, in a place we least expect it—when for a moment our guards are down and we ourselves aren't aware that they're down that much—Satan will come in and reduce us from saint to sinner, from Peter the Rock to Simon the fisherman. At a moment when we feel that we have just about overcome evil, when we feel proud of how much we've grown and changed, sin will find an opportunity to raise its ugly head and show us that there are still gaps in our lives where Satan can pull out our former selves, our former ways, thoughts, and conversation.

And the Lord said, " 'Simon, Simon, behold, Satan hath demanded to have you, that he may sift you like wheat.' In spite of your loyalty, pledge, devotion to me, Satan still wants you. In spite of the way you've served me, Satan still wants you. You've been with me from the beginning and Satan knows how close we are, but Satan still wants you. Don't think that because you're my disciple, Satan has given up hope of claiming your soul. Satan still wants you. Satan wants all who have given themselves to me and I want all, whoever they are and whatever they've done, who have given themselves to Satan. Satan wants you so that you can be used to defeat me; I want you because I love you and want the best for you. Satan wants to sift you as wheat. Satan wants to rub off the grain so that nothing but the chaff remains; I want to save the grain. I want you so that glory, honor, holiness, and praise to almighty God can issue forth out of your life."

"Simon, Simon, behold Satan has desired to have you, that he may sift you as wheat: But I have prayed for thee." In and of ourselves, we are no match for Satan. Let us never delude ourselves into thinking that we are holy enough, righteousness enough, powerful enough to take on Satan by ourselves. No matter how often we've encountered Satan, there are still weapons that we've never seen and tricks that we've never heard of. Although we are no match for Satan, there is no need to fear Satan; we have a Saviour who's praying for us. We have a Savior who's making intercession for us. We have God on our side; we have Christ the Redeemer in our corner; we have the blessed Holy Ghost comforting us when we're troubled and empowering us when we're weak.

Personally I think it's wonderful to know that Jesus is praying for us. There are times when we are so burdened and discouraged that we don't even feel like praying. There are times when Satan has beaten and confused us to the point that we can't seem to get a prayer through. But even then, when we are at our weakest, there is no need to worry—we have a Savior who is praying for us.

God always knows what we're going through because we have a Saviour who constantly lifts our case before heaven's mercy seat. Even when we're not, even when we can't, even when we've forgotten, even when we don't bother—Jesus is still praying for us.

Paul understood the importance of intercessory prayer. That's why he later wrote to the church at Rome: "Likewise the Spirit helps us in our weakness; for we do not know how to pray as we ought, but the Spirit intercedes for us with sighs too deep for words. And he who searches the hearts of men knows what is the mind of the Spirit because the Spirit intercedes for the saints according to the will of God" (Romans 8:26-27). We will never know how far the praying and interceding of others have brought us.

When the Lord spoke, Peter wasn't aware that Satan had such great plans for him. He didn't know that in a few hours the Shepherd would be taken and that the sheep would scatter. He didn't know that very soon he would have to stand by himself and either affirm or deny Christ. He didn't know that, at that very moment, Satan was closer than ever to tearing apart the disciples. He didn't know it, but Jesus did and that's why our Lord had already begun to pray.

It's good to have Jesus praying for us because Jesus sees dangers ahead that we don't even know about. Jesus knows about Satan's plans before we do. Jesus knows that, while we're feeling comfortable, even while we're sleeping, Satan is working, trying to undo us. Jesus knows what Satan will do next and where and how Satan will strike and who Satan will use before we do. We pray for dangers seen but Jesus prays for those unseen. We pray for dangers known but Jesus prays for those unknown. We pray when we get into the situation but Jesus prays before the situation comes upon us.

We don't have to worry about what tomorrow will bring because today Jesus has already prayed for our strength for tomorrow. Jesus saw that mountain that we're afraid to climb before we reached it and has already prayed that we have the strength to climb it; therefore we can climb it in Jesus' name. Jesus is already praying for us to overcome traps, ditches, trials, and burdens unknown to us. We can walk by faith and not by sight because Jesus is praying for us.

It's good to have Jesus pray for us because Jesus knows what to pray for. He told Peter, "I've prayed that your faith fail not."

Many times we don't know what to pray for. Many times we pray for what we really don't need and ought not have. If God gave us all that we prayed for, they would cause our ruin. But Jesus knows just what to ask for. He knows that in a crisis, when the Devil begins to assault us, what we need is faith— faith to hold on until our change comes. In spite of broken health, broken wealth, broken friendships, broken promises, we can make it. If our faith ever fails, we will fall. For "faith is the substance of things hoped for and the evidence of things not seen" (Hebrews 11:1, KJV).

The only thing that kept Job going was faith and trust in God. When he had lost everything, when folks said he had nothing more to live for, it was faith that helped Job lift up his head toward the heavens and say, "Even though I've lost my children, although I've lost my health, wealth, and everything I've owned, I still have a reason for living. For I know that my Redeemer liveth, that he shall stand at the latter day upon the earth; and though these skinworms destroy this body; yet in my flesh shall I see God, whom mine eyes shall behold and not another" (Job 19:25-27, KJV).

It's good to have Jesus pray for us because when Jesus prays, the victory is assured. Jesus told Peter, "I have prayed for you that (above and beyond all else) your faith may not fail, and when (not if, but when) you're converted; when (not if) you survive the onslaught of the devil; when (not if) you find yourself and then find me in the process; when (not if) you gain the victory, strengthen your brothers. You're going to have your ups and downs, your trials and tribulations, but don't worry. I've already given you victory. If you keep your hand in my hand, if you hold onto the profession of your faith without wavering, then don't worry about what the devil does to you or says about you, for I've already given you the victory. Victory belongs to you not because you're so good, righteous, powerful, or smart; victory belongs to you because I've prayed for you" (Luke 22:32, author's paraphrase).

It's good to have Jesus pray for us because wonderful things happen when Jesus prays. Jesus prayed over five barley loaves and two fish one day and five thousand souls were fed. Jesus prayed over the blind and they received their sight. Jesus prayed over the lame and they leaped for joy. Jesus prayed over the deaf and they heard the Good News of a dawning kingdom. Jesus prayed over the dumb and they sang praises to God. Jesus prayed over Lazarus and he received new life. On Calvary one day Jesus prayed, "Father forgive them, for they know not what they do" (Luke 23:34), and my sins and your sins were washed away.

An Easter Faith in a Good Friday World

Matthew 28:11-15

Most of us remember the Watergate scandal which rocked the nation several years ago and created a crisis of credibility regarding faith in government and our elected officials. Watergate is the building where the break-in occurred—where officials tried to obtain some sensitive documents of the Democratic Party. In time, bits and pieces of information began to leak from sources in the White House, and rumors began to circulate that the crime involved persons in high positions within the government, the Republican Party, and even some of the right-hand men of the President of the United States. Much effort was spent in a futile attempt to cover up the trail of this deed and to protect those in high positions who might be implicated. After some intensive investigative reporting, it was discovered that Richard Nixon, the President of the United States, had knowledge of the crime and was implicated in the cover-up. After resigning, he left office in disgrace. Since that time the term "Watergate" has come to mean cover-up and scandal, particularly regarding persons in high places.

Those involved in Watergate tried to cover up the facts and the truth, but found it impossible to do so. They tried to live as if certain things had not happened and certain realities were not the case, but in the end they were not able to do so.

In the Old Testament, we are told about another scandal of

Watergate proportions that occurred during the reign of David as king of Israel. David plotted to have Uriah, one of his soldiers, killed in battle so that he could marry Uriah's wife, Bathsheba, with whom he was romantically involved and who was carrying David's child. With the death of Uriah, David thought he had covered up his misdeeds, but Nathan, the prophet, implicated David and delivered God's word of judgment upon him.

Our text informs us of another effort to cover up the truth which is more dastardly and despicable than any we have discussed. According to Matthew's Gospel, when Jesus was crucified, the religious leaders remembered his promise to rise again. They did not believe Jesus' promise, so they said, but they feared that our Lord's disciples would be as devious regarding the resurrection promise as they had been in the execution of the crucifixion plan. Consequently, to prevent the disciples from stealing the Lord's body from its resting place, they asked Pilate to secure the tomb against theft. Pilate appointed soldiers to guard the tomb and told them to secure it as best they could. They sealed the entrance with a stone and stationed a guard. Like David and the Watergate criminals, they secured truth and righteousness in the tomb as best they could.

Sooner or later we are going to learn that there is no human security system against truth, righteousness, and the promises of God. No pack of lies can bury truth forever; no amount of wrongdoing can bury goodness and righteousness forever; no earthly power can prevent God's promises from coming forth in the fullness of time.

Toward the dawn of the first day of the week, Mary Magdalene and another Mary went to the sepulchre and, on time according to the plan of heaven, there was an earthquake in the vicinity of the tomb where Jesus was buried. "An angel of the Lord descended from heaven and rolled back the stone and sat upon it. His appearance was like lightning and his raiment white as snow; and for fear of him the guards trembled and [fainted]" (Matthew 28:2-4).

The women, who had come with spices to anoint their Lord's dead body, stood still as the fierce, armed, male guards fainted. Though powerfully armed and equipped with the weapons of this world, we cannot stand when the word of Christ begins to be fulfilled, when righteousness is resurrected from the tomb where it has been buried. The angels told the women of Jesus' resurrection and instructed them to go and tell the disciples that their Lord was risen from the dead.

As the women went their way, some of the soldiers went to the city and told the chief priests what had happened. The priests then assembled with some of their cohorts and planned to enter into deception. After some discussion among themselves, they decided to bribe the soldiers with money and have them tell the people that the disciples came by night and stole the body while they slept. If word came to Pilate, then intercession would be made on behalf of the soldiers to keep them out of trouble. According to the Scriptures, the soldiers took the money and did as they had been directed.

The bribery of the soldiers was only one more act of dishonesty among a number of others in the plot by the religious leaders to discredit and destroy Jesus. When one looks at the way they had already lied and connived, threatened and intimidated to destroy Jesus, one is not surprised that these "men of God" would stoop to bribery. After all, they had bribed one of Jesus' disciples to betray him. From the beginning, in the initial stages of the plot to stop Jesus, they had compromised themselves.

There is no right way or good way to do wrong. Wrongdoing involves compromise at the very outset. It means starting out on the wrong foot, which means that every other step we take will be heading in the wrong direction. The journey of wrongdoing doesn't get any better as we go along but goes from bad to worse.

Instead of having open ears to hear what God was saying or accepting the evidences of God's Spirit and power at work in Jesus' life, the religious leaders were jealous of Jesus and threatened by Jesus, causing them to look at Jesus with a critical eye.

Whenever jealousy and insecurity are at the root of our actions, we've already started off on the wrong foot. The religious leaders' critical eyes prompted them to try to discredit Jesus. When their criticism proved to be of no avail; when our Lord constantly shot holes in their criticism and left them speechless, they began to plot his downfall.

Treachery was used to seize Jesus. These "righteous" men encouraged Judas, one of the Lord's disciples, to betray him. They tried him illegally. These righteous men broke all the laws which they held sacred and which were supposed to govern the conduct of the Sanhedrin, their high court, to convict the Lord. They used slander to charge him before Pontius Pilate. They made up a charge which had no truth in it so that Pilate might judge him. They used threats to force a sentence. When Pilate wanted to clear Jesus, they threatened to report Pilate as incompetent and disloyal to Caesar. They opted for the release of a criminal in order to detain him. When Pilate offered to release a prisoner according to the custom of the Passover season and gave them a choice of Barabbas, the thief, or Jesus, the Son of God, they chose Barabbas. They used cruelty to kill him. They asked that he be crucified—the most painful and disgraceful means of death they had. And now in our text, they are once again using bribery to cover up the truth. They were still living in a Good Friday world.

Good Friday was humanity's darkest day. When one thinks of how unjust the crucifixion was, one could easily get the impression that might makes right, that justice is a joke, goodness a farce, and that righteousness is of no consequence. When one looks at Good Friday, one could get the impression that God's face had been turned away from the creation and we had been left to the reign and machinations of human beings who had the power to manipulate and control our destinies to fit their selfish purposes. When one looks at Good Friday, one could get the impression that money and power control human destiny.

Good Friday tells us that bribery and corruption rule this world. Good Friday tells us that we are the masters of our fate and the captains of our souls and that we can do whatever we are big enough to do without fear of consequences as long as we have money to buy our way or power to force our way. There are people and nations who act as if this is still a Good Friday world.

The religious establishment of Jesus' day was trying to perpetrate one of the biggest hoaxes ever played on humanity. It was a hoax as big as the one Satan played on Adam and Eve in the Garden of Eden when Satan told them that if they disobeyed God's word and ate of the forbidden fruit, they would be as smart as God. When our first parents fell for Satan's trick, the human spirit and human destiny became enslaved to the power of sin. The hoax that those in our text were trying to perpetrate was that we, as humans, were still hopelessly bound by sin. They wanted us to believe that the sin of Eden which fashioned Good Friday triumphed, and that the Good Friday world of sin and violence was still intact. There are those who act as if nothing happened beyond Good Friday to change the reign of sin and violence.

Some of us, however, have come to declare that the hoax didn't work. The soldiers may have sold out, but the women who carried the good news of the resurrection didn't become sidetracked. Jesus was not stopped from appearing to the women and telling them, "Do not be afraid; go tell my brethren to go to Galilee, and there they will see me" (Matthew 28:10).

Jesus was not prevented from appearing to his disciples as they assembled in fear and saying, "Peace be with you." This is not a Good Friday world; this is the world of the risen Christ who beat back the powers of darkness and is alive forevermore. "Peace be with you!" (John 20:19). Jesus was not detained from leading his followers to a high mountain where he told them, "All authority in heaven and on earth has been given to me. Go therefore and make disciples of all nations, baptizing them in the name of the Father and of the Son and of the Holy Spirit, teaching them to observe all that I have commanded you; and lo, I am with you always, to the close of the age" (Matthew 28:18-20).

While some may live as if this world is governed by the darkness of Good Friday, we have come to declare that something has superceded Good Friday. It is an Easter faith which rejoices in the reality of a risen Lord—a Lord of hope, love, justice, forgiveness, a Lord of might and mercy, repentance and salvation. Jesus is Calvary's hero, the grave spoiler, and death's conqueror. Never believe that wrong will last forever or that Satan will always abuse the saints. Our Easter faith tells us that right, hope, justice, and peace have not been defeated and that, not only are they alive, but in Jesus they reign forevermore. If having an Easter faith means anything, it means that we have a reason for hoping and a reason for rejoicing, in spite of the continued existence of sin.

There was an old lady who used to come to church and rejoice every Sunday. If the preaching was good she rejoiced and if the preaching was bad she rejoiced. If the singing was good she rejoiced and if the singing was bad she rejoiced. One day one of her children asked her why she rejoiced all the time, no matter how good or bad the services were. She said, "If the preaching and singing are good then I feel good and I rejoice. And if the preaching and singing are bad then I look beyond the preacher and the singer and see Jesus, and keep on rejoicing."

If having an Easter faith means anything, it means we can look beyond Good Friday sin, Good Friday hopelessness, Good Friday violence, Good Friday injustice, Good Friday corruption, Good Friday cruelty, and see Jesus reigning above it all—and keep on rejoicing.

An Easter faith in a Good Friday world means we can look beyond South Africa, Nicaragua, and look beyond tensions in the Middle East, tensions between Russia and the United States, look beyond tensions between black and white and rich and poor, and see Jesus reigning as the Lord of history and the Prince of Peace—and keep on rejoicing. We can look beyond problems and see Jesus reigning as a problem solver—and keep on rejoicing. We can look beyond unemployment and see Jesus reigning with power to "make a way somehow"—and keep on rejoicing. We can look beyond sickness and see Jesus reigning as the Lord of life and the door to eternal life—and keep on rejoicing. We can look beyond death and see Jesus reigning as the resurrection and the life—and keep on rejoicing.

Jesus Keeps Hanging Around

1 Corinthians 15:5–8

When I read this passage of Scripture I am struck by the number of appearances that Jesus made as the resurrected Christ of faith and the triumphant Lord of history before his ascension to his Father and our God. One could raise the question as to why he hung around so long. After all, he had done that which he came to do.

He had preached the Good News of God's steadfast love and provision for those who were economically and/or spiritually poor. He had brought release to those who were held captive to a religious legalism that neither saved nor satisfied. He had brought sight to those who had never seen and returned vision to those who had lost it. He had given those who were oppressed the liberating assurance of their own self-worth. He had announced that the kingdom of heaven was at hand and had transformed a bleak present to the acceptable year of the Lord. He had healed the sick, raised the dead, and cast out demons. He had made the ultimate sacrifice by allowing humans to misuse him, abuse him, and crucify him so that they could be redeemed. On the cross of Calvary, in his dying hour, Jesus had pronounced his work "finished."

One would expect, then, that after some initial appearances to establish his victory over death, hell, and the grave, Jesus would have immediately ascended to his Father. One would expect Jesus to be anxious about his imminent return and be in a hurry to leave this sinful world with its fickle humans and their cruel acts and return to the joy, peace, and glory of heaven.

However, according to our text, Jesus took his time about his ascension. He seemed in no hurry to leave this terrestrial plain. He appeared to Cephas, better known as Peter, and then to the Twelve. He was seen by more than five hundred believers at one time. James saw him, as did the other apostles. Last of all, long after the others, he was seen by Paul as one born almost too late. Jesus just simply kept hanging around.

He appeared to his good friend Peter, who, before the others, had recognized him as the Christ, the Son, the incarnate embodiment of the living God. He appeared to Peter who had pledged eternal devotion, but who, in his hour of testing, seemed to be more a broken reed than a rock man. He hung around long enough to restore a fallen saint, to lift the spirits of a downcast friend, to forgive the denial of a trusted follower, and to reclaim as his very own one whose faith Satan had tried to break and whose soul the Evil One desired to sift like wheat.

Jesus always hangs around for saints who stumble. When others criticize us for stumbling, when our weaknesses and failures seem to mock our faith, when our adversaries seem to have gotten the victory, and when our consciences have beaten and shamed us, Jesus hangs around long enough to let us know that he loves us just the same. Regardless of our broken promises and shattered resolves, he still claims us as his own. Jesus hangs around long enough to let us know that, though our sins be as scarlet, his blood can still make the foulest clean, that we are forgiven, and can still walk in the newness of life. Jesus keeps hanging around.

Jesus hung around long enough to appear to the Twelve. He appeared to those whom he had called by name to drop their nets, leave tax collecting tables, and give up all to become itinerant heralds of the dawning kingdom.

Theirs was a unique place in the emergence of the faith. No other humans before or after them would have the privilege of knowing the Master in such an intimate and personal way. It had been their privilege to see and hear things that the prophets and others gone before had longed to behold.

They were the leadership nucleus of the movement. Coming generations would depend upon the accuracy of their recollections and writings for the appropriation and distillation of the faith. The movement would expand or dissipate, live or die, based upon their efforts.

Because much had been given unto them, much would be required. Because they were the leaders, they would be the first to die when the church was persecuted. They would be used as examples of what could happen to a person who openly confessed Christ as Lord. When the Master was crucified, each of them had been gripped by a deep and painful sense of personal loss and tragedy. However, our text tells us that before his ascension, Jesus hung around long enough to appear to the Twelve.

Let us never forget that Jesus always hangs around for those from whom much is required. There are always those who bear more than what seems their fair share of burdens, who experience more than their share of suffering, and who carry more than their share of responsibility. There are those whose lives have more than their share of setbacks, problems, tragedies, or misfortunes. There are those whose bodies endure more than their share of frustrating sickness and demoralizing pain.

There are those upon whose shoulders the mantles of leadership and responsibility rests like a heavy yoke. They have enough responsibility for two or three persons. As children, they must grow up faster and assume adult responsibilities for providing and caring for the rest of the family. As single persons, they have to be both mother and father to children; both husband and wife to hold homes together; both son and daughter for aged parents and other lonely persons. Sometimes their shoulders begin to ache from the weight of the crosses upon their backs, and they begin to wonder if they can bear up, how long they can stand the strain of leadership and responsibility for self, for family, for livelihood, for bills, for trying to stand right.

The message of the text, however, is that Jesus hangs around to comfort, empower, and preserve those from whom much is required. If we go on in Jesus name, according to his Word, we will never walk alone. Jesus is always with them and us—he just keeps hanging around.

Jesus hung around long enough to appear to five hundred believing Christians. Jesus kept hanging around until he was seen by the church as a whole. He did not simply appear to the leadership cadre, or those who held special positions or offices, those who were ordained to certain orders, or to those who had been endowed with special gifts. He was seen by the whole church.

Jesus understood that it takes more than the leadership to do the work of the kingdom—it takes the whole church. In his appearance before the five hundred, Jesus demonstrated his lordship, ownership, care, and commitment to the whole church. Jesus was not simply Peter's Lord or Lord of the Twelve, but Lord of the whole church. Jesus is not simply Lord of those who belong to a certain clique or club—he is Lord of the whole church. Jesus is not simply Lord for those whose names are always being called or just for those whose names and families go back to the beginning—he is Lord of the whole church. Jesus is not simply Lord of those who give the most or talk the most—he is Lord of the whole church.

We believe in the priesthood of all believers. We believe that the same gifts that are bestowed upon some, the same spiritual experiences which happen to some, the same spiritual depths achieved by some, are available to all. We believe that God is no respecter of persons and that each of us carries within ourselves a believing heart, a faith line that reaches the throne of grace.

Consequently, the presence of the risen Lord is as available to the so-called newcomer as he is to the so-called "church pillar." Jesus is as available to the poorest as he is to the most prosperous, to the disabled as well as the healthy of body and mind, to women as well as men.

Jesus' appearance before five hundred believing Christians demonstrates the truth that wherever God's children are doing the work of the kingdom and calling on the name of the Lord, Jesus will be there—hanging around, reclaiming the backslider, strengthening the weak, confirming the faith of those who doubt, saving to the uttermost, anointing anew, and baptizing with the Holy Ghost. When it comes to the life and well-being of God's church—not ours but God's—Jesus keeps hanging around.

Jesus hung around long enough to appear to his brother, James. One of the most discouraging and painful experiences of Jesus' life must have centered around the coolness, disbelief, and rejection from many in his family toward his mission. When Jesus went back to Nazareth, after doing mighty works in Capernaum and other places and met the hostility, mockery, and disbelief of his home community, his comment that a prophet is not without honor except in his own land and among his own kinsmen was not just a reference to neighbors and distance relations, but also a reference to his own brothers and sisters.

Family, friends, and those closest to us can hurt us in a way that no one else can. Jesus' family didn't understand him. To some, he was as crazy and as eccentric as his cousin, John the Baptist. To others he was an embarrassment and to still others he was a mystery. Sometimes, when God begins to move in our lives in special ways, those closest to us will not understand. However, we cannot afford to sacrifice our convictions or the joy of the Lord because of the lack of understanding, or hang-ups, or lack of vision of others. We must be prepared to let nothing, including the approval or disapproval of those whom we love, separate us from the love of God.

However, sometimes we can accomplish in death what we cannot achieve in life. Sometimes it's only in the afterglow of a sainted life that has passed from our midst that we can appreciate all that that person stood for and all that they tried to teach us. Often we would love to have told that person how grateful we were for his or her life and how much he or she really meant to us, but by then it is too late.

Perhaps James had been one of those who had rejected Jesus when he went back home to Nazareth. However, as time passed, perhaps toward the close of the Master's ministry, James began to understand the nature of the kingdom that his older brother had been talking about. James had marvelled at how his brother had prayed for the forgiveness of his enemies when he was on the cross. James may have regretted that he hadn't done more to support Jesus while he lived and now that his brother was dead, he may have felt it was too late—his opportunities for service had passed him by. But according to the Scriptures, Jesus hung around long enough for James to see him, giving James the assurance that it wasn't too late.

Jesus keeps hanging around to let us know that it's never too late. Even now, at our ages and stations in life—regardless of what we've done or failed to do—it's not too late. As long as there is breath in our bodies and we can call on the name of Jesus, it's not too late. Now is still the acceptable time. Now is still the day of salvation. This day can be the first day of the rest of your life because Jesus is still hanging around.

Not only did Jesus hang around for Peter and the Twelve, for the five hundred, and for James, but he hung around long enough for a young Pharisee whose name was Saul to meet him. This young man wasn't around when the Lord called Peter and the others to follow him. He wasn't around when Christ appeared to the five hundred. He didn't have the privilege of growing up with Jesus from childhood like James.

It was long after the others had encountered the risen Christ that one day, while he was on the Damascus Road on his way to wreak havoc on the church, Saul discovered that Jesus was still hanging around. At midday he saw a blinding light and heard a voice from heaven that called him by name and asked, "Saul, Saul why are you persecuting me?" When Saul asked, "Who are you Lord?" the voice replied, "I am Jesus of Nazareth, the once dead but now living and exalted Lord. And it is not good for you to fight the work of the kingdom." From that day,

Paul's life took on a new direction.

That same Jesus who spoke to Paul is still hanging around. Jesus' grace is still sufficient, his strength is still perfected in our weakness, his arm of compassion has not been shortened, his love has not abated, his mercy is still from everlasting to everlasting, his blood still sanctifies, and his spirit still sets free. Jesus' forgiveness is still stronger than sin, his joy is mightier than the ocean, his peace still passes understanding, and his salvation is still stronger than death.

I know Jesus is still hanging around because one day I met him for myself. I come from a tradition where people used to say, "I looked at my hands and my hands looked new; I looked at my feet and they did too; I looked all around me and all around me shined; I asked the Lord, 'was all this mine?' "

The Spirit Brings Life

Acts 2:1–4

There is a legend that states that after the ascension—when Jesus returned to heaven as the exalted and reigning Christ—some of the angels, archangels, and others of the heavenly host were curious about his earthly sojourn and questioned him about his accomplishments.

They asked, "Did you found a great movement? Did you lead a great army? How many followers did you have?" To which our Lord replied, "I generally attracted good crowds, but I only had twelve disciples and a few friends and dedicated followers."

"Well," they said, "if there were so few they must have been exceptional human beings with sterling characters, persons who were leaders in their communities and successful in their careers." To this Jesus replied, "Actually they were rather ordinary—a tax collector, several fishermen, just common working people."

"Evidently they must have been a very loyal group," the others said. Jesus answered, "I believe they wanted to be loyal, but in my hour of crisis one betrayed me, another denied me, and almost all of them fled."

"And yet you expect this group to carry on your work?" they asked. "Yes I do!" Jesus said.

"Surely," they said, "you have some alternative plan." "No," said Jesus, "I have no alternative plan."

"But you must have another group in reserve somewhere in the event this one fails," the angels said. To which Jesus replied, "I have no other group. This group is the only one that I am depending upon, because this group is my church."

As unstable, and as unreliable as we are, as easily as we become discouraged or distracted, as quickly as we become tired and ready to give up, as often as we are inclined to complain and engage in self-pity, as stubborn as we are and as insistent in walking in our own willful ways, as weak and as unworthy as we are, the fact remains that Christ has committed and entrusted the ongoing work of the kingdom into our hands.

Any casual reading of the New Testament will reveal that our Lord left his work in some very shaky hands. It was left in the hands of disciples who demonstrated time and time again that they were unworthy of it and should not be trusted with it. To the very end, Peter continued to leap before he looked and speak before he thought. To the end, Judas maintained a secret agenda while Thomas openly voiced his skepticism. To the end, Philip continued to ask inane questions while James and John tried to plot and politic their way to the two top spots in the kingdom. Yet these were the ones who had been entrusted with the task of proclaiming salvation to a lost and wayward world.

The church that Christ left was a disappointed church. Those whom the Master called had a different conception and different expectations of his messiahship than he did. They expected him to inaugurate an earthly kingdom and they saw themselves on earthly thrones. They had hoped that he would redeem Israel, but his teachings, coupled with Calvary, had shattered their hopes.

The church that Christ left was a confused church. How could Jesus allow himself to be crucified? They had seen him rebuke raging storms, cast out demons, heal the sick, and raise the dead. They knew that he could have withstood Caiaphas' vindictiveness, Herod's arrogance, and Pilate's vacillation.

They knew he could have called legions of angels to fight his battles. So why would he submit to Calvary?

Their confusion was the confusion of all of the faithful when they see goodness abused and crucified at the hands of evil, or when life seems to contradict all that they believe about a just and powerful and good God.

The church that Christ left was a weakened church. Their fellowship had been decimated by divisions, betrayals, desertions, and denials. Satan had shown that all of them were disciples with clay feet and that none of them could be counted on when the chips were down. All of them had been shamed by their behavior on the night that Jesus was betrayed and none of them could feel quite the same about themselves when they looked in the mirror. Their self-confidence, their perception of who and what they were had been shaken.

The church that Christ left was a frightened church. It was a church that hid itself behind drawn shutters and closed doors. Now that Jesus had been crucified, what would happen to them? Jesus had already told them that the servant was not greater than his or her master, nor the messenger greater than the sender. Jesus had already told them that if the world hated and rejected him it would also hate and reject them. Having seen what happened to Jesus, they feared for their own lives.

The church that Jesus left was a lifeless church. It was a church in mourning. They had lost the physical presence of the One who was their integrating center. They had lost the One who had called them from where they were and brought them together. They had lost the One who had given them life.

The church that Christ left was all of this, to be sure, but it was also more than this. The church that Christ left was also a believing church, a hopeful church, a trusting church, an expecting church. With all that had happened to their little group, with all of their disappointment, confusion, weakness, fear, and personal loss, they still dared to believe Christ's promises and follow his commands. There were some things that Satan couldn't destroy and the world couldn't touch. There were some things they could still trust, and Christ's promises ranked among them.

It is said that once the great violinist, Nicolo Paganini, was in concert when one of the strings on his instrument broke. The crowd laughed. He continued to play, however, and shortly afterward another string broke. The crowd laughed again. Later, when the third string broke and Paganini continued to bring forth glorious music from the one string left, the audience looked on in hushed wonder. They realized they were indeed in the presence of a master who could bring forth sublime music from a violin with three broken strings.

The church that Christ left had three broken strings but they continued to play on the one string of their faith which was left—the promises of Christ. The Lord had promised them a comforter; he had promised them power, and they had never known Christ to lie.

When they thought about it, they remembered that Jesus had told them that this time would come. He told them that he would be rejected, and that he would suffer and be killed. Jesus told them that when the Shepherd was stricken, the sheep would scatter. Jesus told them that they would have tribulation in this world but to be of good cheer, for he had overcome the world. Early on that third morning, while it was still dark, Jesus rose just as he said he would. Christ had always kept his word. Therefore, in spite of all that had happened, the disciples continued to believe.

Sometimes all we have to go on is our experience in trusting God's Word. Sometimes life, circumstances, and reality will contradict all that we believe; sometimes we won't know what the future holds; at times the only string we have left is our knowledge of what Jesus has done—how he has stood with us, fought battles for us, and opened doors for us. But if we can just play on that one string, if we can remember that the Lord has always kept his promises and that he has promised to be with us, it gives us reason to keep hoping and trusting, praying and believing.

The church that Jesus left, therefore, assembled together during the time of year when the Jews observed the festival known as the Feast of Weeks or Pentecost. Pentecost means "fifty days" and it was celebrated on the fiftieth day after the beginning of the Jewish Passover. It was essentially an agricultural feast where the Jews presented unto the Lord the first-fruits of their labors. However, it later came to be associated with the reading of the Law because it was believed that Moses received the law at Mt. Sinai and delivered it to the people on the fiftieth day after the angel of death had passed through Egypt slaying the firstborn of Egyptian households to secure the release of God's people from slavery.

Jesus had been crucified during the Passover season. He had walked among his disciples for forty days after his resurrection and then for ten days the church had gathered in an upper room to receive the promise. It had been fifty days since their Lord had been crucified and the promise had not yet come, but still they believed. Sometimes, simply to assemble together in expectation is an act of faith in and of itself.

Thus, when the Day of Pentecost was fully come, on the fiftieth day, when Jews customarily assembled in the synagogue and temple to hear the Law read, the Spirit baptized the church with power. On the day when the Law had been lifted up, the Spirit established itself as the guiding force and power in the life of the church.

Let us never forget that Christ not only keeps his promises, but also that his promises are perfectly timed. Sometimes we try to hurry the Lord to deliver before the proper time. Sometimes we think that the Lord has moved too late or after the proper time. But the Lord always moves on time and his promises are always kept in perfect time. My mother used to tell me, "He might not come when you want him, but he always comes on time."

When the Spirit came the saints were assembled. They were not scattered hither and yon with one doing his or her grief thing over here and another doing his or her guilt thing over there. They were in one place. Even in a weakened church we must never underestimate the power which can come to saints when they assemble themselves together in Jesus' name. It is said that a group of tribal chieftains were in council and each had his own plan for meeting a threatened attack. An old and wise chief gave each a single stick and told him to break it. Each did so without difficulty. Gathering the same number of sticks again, the old chief bound them together into a bundle. He passed it to each of the other chiefs and told them to break it. Not even the strongest was able to do so. God gave us to each other because we need each other. There is still power in the communion of saints. There is still more power in a weak church than there is in a strong individual. Individually, no matter how strong we think we are, we can be broken. But when we come together and stay together, even when we are at our weakest, not even the gates of hell can prevail against us.

Not only was the church in one place, but when the Holy Spirit came it was also of one accord. It is possible for the church to assemble in a spirit of discord. When the church assembles with a contrary spirit, it can lose its identity as the church because it begins to act and talk like everybody else. But when the church is in unity, when the church is in a spirit of love, when the church is in one accord in its spirit, it can really be the church because then the Holy Spirit can flow most freely.

"And when the day of Pentecost was fully come, they were all with one accord in one place. And suddenly . . ." We can't program or time the Holy Spirit. We can't work it up or bring it in. We can't turn it on at will and turn it off at whim. We may be able to do all of that with our spirit but not with the Holy Spirit. For the Holy Ghost is like the wind; it blows where it wills and we hear the sound thereof. We are moved by its force and refreshed by its breeze, but we can't tell from whence it comes or whither it goes. The Spirit comes of its own accord— suddenly—and falls where it wills. The only thing we can do is prepare ourselves to receive it when and if it comes. Our job is to make sure that the setting is conducive to its coming and that we are real and sincere in asking it to come.

On the day of Pentecost, when the church was in one place and of one accord, suddenly the Holy Ghost came. When the

Spirit came, four things happened to the church: they heard, they saw, they were filled, and they spoke.

They heard a sound from heaven as of a "rushing mighty wind" that filled all the house where they were assembled. They looked and over the heads of everyone they saw cloven tongues of fire. They saw fire—fires of clearing and cleansing, destruction and purification, melting and kindling, burning up and burning through. And they were all filled with the Holy Ghost. Two bodies can't occupy the same space at the same time, thus, when they were filled with the Holy Ghost their disappointment gave way to joy, their confusion to clear perception, their weakness to strength, their fear to courage, their loss to life.

The Spirit gave them new life and they spoke in other tongues as the Spirit gave them utterance. The tongues in which they spoke were not gibberish, but intelligible languages.

It so happened that Jerusalem was filled that day with persons from all over the world who were there to celebrate the Jewish Pentecost. When they heard the shouts of praise from the one church of one accord in the one Holy Spirit, they understood what was said, for they asked: "How can this be? These men are all from Galilee, and yet we hear them speaking in our various native tongues. We hear them in our own native language proclaiming the mighty works of God." And, when they sought the meaning of it all, there were those in the crowd who tried to make light of the Spirit's work by saying they were just drunk from drinking new wine.

There will always be those who will not understand or appreciate or choose not to be a part of the movement of the Holy Spirit. There will always be those who will try to throw water on the fire, but if one truly has been anointed with the fire that falls from above, God will give an answer and the holy boldness to proclaim it.

Peter stood up and said they were not drunk—it was only nine o'clock in the morning—too early to be drunk. "This is that which was spoken by the prophet Joel," he said. " 'And it shall come to pass in the last days, saith God,' 'I will pour out my Spirit upon all flesh [not just bishops, elders, priests, deacons, licentiates, evangelists—but all flesh; not just leading lay people, big names, big givers, church pillars, leading families, but all flesh; not just adults, children, the elderly, but all flesh; not just the rich, the educated, the privileged, the mighty, but all flesh] and your sons and daughters shall prophesy and your young men shall see visions and your old men shall dream dreams. . . . It shall come to pass that whosoever shall call on the name of the Lord shall be saved.' "

When Peter finished preaching under the power of the Spirit, three thousand souls were added to the kingdom. In one day the church increased by three thousand. The Spirit does bring life.

John Bunyan once saw in a vision a man throwing water on a flame of fire and yet the flame continued to burn. He wondered how it could keep on burning until he saw there was someone behind the door pouring oil on the flame.

I'm so glad that when this world tries to drown our fires, the Holy Spirit is there to keep putting oil on the flames. Sometimes I feel discouraged and it seems like my work and my living are in vain, but then the Holy Spirit revives my soul again. In those moments of testing and trial I've learned to pray like the hymn writer:

> Spirit of the living God, fall afresh on me;
> Spirit of the living God, fall afresh on me.
> Break me, melt me, mold me, fill me.
> Spirit of the living God, fall afresh on me.

How Deep Is Your Religion?

Ezekiel 47:1–5 (LB)

Many of us view the new year as a time of beginning afresh, of setting new goals for ourselves, and of making changes in our patterns of living. Some of us began the new year by saying to ourselves, as well as to others, "I'm going to do things differently this year. I'm going to make some needed changes that I've been neglecting for too long. I'm going to be a different person than I have been in the past." Others of us don't see ourselves making too many radical changes in our lives, no drastic alterations from the previous year. Though everything in our lives is not perfect, we are basically satisfied and reasonably content. Last year wasn't that bad for us so we just hope that things will go on as before, that we will continue in the way that we've been heading.

Whether we see ourselves making many or few changes, we all have at least one goal in common. Every one of us, from the youngest to the oldest, from the richest to the poorest, from the least to the most educated, from the most pious to the most worldly, should have this as our goal. Each of us needs to strive for more depth in the Lord and more growth in God's grace. Our prayers and goal should be that at the end of the year we find ourselves stronger in the Lord, with more depth in the Spirit, more understanding of God's Word, more commitment to doing God's will. As we are all aware, there are still unplumbed depths in the Lord that we haven't yet reached and there are heights of joy that we haven't yet attained. The Spirit of God ought not be finished with any of us yet. No matter how much we have experienced or think we know, there is still much that God's Spirit can teach and reveal to us.

The Christian journey is something that we must grow into. One does not reach the highest heights or deepest depths by wishing it or wanting it or claiming it. I try not to judge anyone's religion, but I become suspect of people who become holy and sanctified overnight. Such people often come in to the Christian life with a bang and go out with a whimper. Rather than waning and weakening with time, true religion proceeds from strength to strength. Time takes its toll on all we know and everything we use except religion and our faith.

In time, the clothes we wear, no matter how fine or expensive they are, wear out. In time, the cars we drive wear out; their bodies rust out and their engines stop running. In time, the houses we live in begin to weaken and crumble. In time, the art equipment we purchase becomes outdated and obsolete. In time, our own bodies deteriorate. In time, the greatest of athletes lose their coordination and must retire. In time, the vitality of youth wanes as our steps slow and our energy fades. In time, stars noted for their beauty and whose names were once household words fade from public memory. In time, even the caskets in which we are buried, no matter how much we've paid for them, rot away to dust. The Christian, however, gets stronger with time. Only the Christian can say, "Though our outer nature is wasting away, our inner nature is being renewed every day." The Christian life should go from strength to strength and glory to glory. Every round should go higher and higher. Each victory ought to help us "some other to win."

There should be a difference between my religion now and the religion I had when I first started preaching. My faith ought to be stronger; I ought to have more depth and knowledge. I shouldn't be discouraged as easily or willing to quit so readily; my feelings should not be hurt as quickly. I should be more convinced and convicted about the reality and truth of some things now. I should be more firm and resolute about some things and more flexible about other things now. Life, the church, people, God, the Scriptures, the world should not look the same now as they did twenty-six years ago when I first started preaching. If everything and everybody looks the same now as they did then, I haven't grown very much. Growth makes one see things differently.

I'm not simply talking about the passage of time, because the years can go by without much growth taking place. Some people still think the same thoughts, talk the same way about the same people and the same things, and try to do the same things they did many years ago. Therefore, each of us needs to look at ourselves at the beginning of the new year and see how much or how little we have grown in grace, in the Spirit, in the knowledge of God since last year. At the beginning of each year each of us needs to look not at our neighbor but at ourselves to see how much depth we have in God so that we can grow in the fullness and knowledge of the Lord as the Holy Spirit directs.

In Ezekiel's vision recounted in our text, the land was nourished by a stream of water that flowed from the temple. As Ezekiel walked along the banks of the stream he was directed at certain intervals to step into the water to ascertain its depth. At one point the water was ankle deep, and at another point he was knee deep in the stream. He followed the stream a little further, and the next time he stepped into the stream he was waist deep. When he stepped into the water a little further downstream, he discovered that the stream had become a river so deep that he could not stand up and cross it on foot; he had to swim across. At the beginning of this new year each of us should ask ourselves, "How deep is our religion?"

Some of us have ankle-deep religion. Walking through water that is ankle deep is generally no problem and requires a minimum of adjustment on our part. All we have to do is take off our shoes, roll up our trousers or hems a bit, and we can easily move through ankle-deep water. It is so shallow we can easily run through it. After we come out of it and roll down our pants, lower our hems, and put on our shoes, people can't even tell we've been in the water. Some of us have ankle-deep religion. It doesn't inconvenience us much; we only have to make a minimum adjustment. We occasionally go to church or we may attend regularly provided we are not inconvenienced too much. Our pace is hardly slowed. We can still curse people as quickly; we can still drink as much and clown as much as before. All we have to do is take off a couple hours a week to run through some church service. We don't have to change our way of living or talking. We don't want church services to last too long or become too spiritual; we don't want to be challenged about our stewardship and discipleship.

We want a convenient religion that we can run into and out of quickly. We are in and out of it so quickly that most people see no difference in us at all. We're still "hell" to live with at home, cantankerous on the job, and cross in our daily contact with people. Even church people in the same stream with us can't see any growth or difference in us, because there isn't any. That's the trouble with ankle-deep religion; it may be convenient, but it doesn't last. It dries up as quickly as the water we wipe off of our feet. When we need it, we don't have it, because it has dried out. We didn't stay in the stream long enough and go deep enough to become saturated by the waters of the Spirit.

There are others who have knee-deep religion. Knee-deep religion is not quite as convenient as ankle-deep religion. It slows us down a little more than ankle-deep religion does, some, but not too much. We can run through water when it's ankle-deep and walk through it when it's knee deep. Knee-deep religion inconveniences us some but not much. We can still keep on the same clothes; we just have to roll up our pants and lift our hems a little higher. The difference between knee-deep and ankle-deep religion is a matter of convenience. When we have ankle-deep religion we aren't inconvenienced at all; when we have knee-deep religion, we don't mind being inconvenienced some but not much. Some of us want *some* religion but not much. We want *some* of the Holy Spirit but not much—not so much that we can't control it; not so much that we might have to change. We don't mind giving up some of our substance but not much; we'll tip the Lord or give God the left-overs, but we certainly don't want to give God the tithe, the minimum ten percent which the Scriptures call for. We'll give some service, but not much. We'll serve on some committees and work on some projects provided they don't take too much of our time.

People with knee-deep religion are like the members of the church at Laodicea in the book of Revelation whom the risen Lord said were neither hot nor cold but lukewarm. Our Lord condemned lukewarm religion. While knee-deep religion calls for some commitment, renders some service, possesses some love of God and zeal of the Spirit, it will not save us. When trouble comes and problems arise, it isn't deep enough to hold us. When we become discouraged and feel like giving up, it can't hold us fast. When the adversary attacks, knee-deep religion is not deep enough to shield us. Knee-deep religion cannot unlock the deep mysteries and sweetest joys of the faith. It's just not deep enough. Just like we can get out of ankle-deep religion, we can also get out of knee-deep religion and walk away from it as easily as we walked into it, wearing the same clothes and looking and acting the same way.

Ezekiel walked a little farther along the banks of the stream until he was directed to step into it again. This time when he stepped into the stream, the water came to his waist. Waist-high religion requires greater commitment than the others. We have to go a little farther to get it and we can't get out of it as easily. We can run through ankle-deep water and walk through knee-deep water, but when it becomes waist deep all we can do is wade through it. Waist-high religion has some depth to it. When water comes to our waists, we cannot hide the fact that we have been in the water because the lower half of our bodies has been totally immersed. The tops of our bodies may be dry but we still must change garments because the lower halves have been well soaked. When we have waist-high religion, we have had sufficient experience with Christ and the Spirit to have some changes take place in our lives. Even though there are areas that have remained dry, places where the work of the gospel and the Spirit have not taken hold, much of our living has been submitted to Christ. And although people will notice the dry areas, they also see how wet we are and admit that at some point we must have had some type of experience with Jesus. We are so thoroughly wet that we must put on different garments, the robes of righteousness, and acquire a different look.

Most of us are waist high in our religious quest. That's where most of our members, officers, and preachers are found. For most of us our commitments to our God, our faith, and our church are strong enough that we can't simply run away or walk away from them. So we spend our lives slowly wading through this tedious journey—waist deep in the Spirit, waist deep in grace, waist deep in the love of God, waist deep in the Word of God, waist deep in Christ. It's not as easy to pull somebody out of the waters when they are waist deep as it is when they are ankle or knee deep in it. Most of us are firm and secure in our religious commitment, and it serves most of our purposes. No matter who comes or who goes we're going to stay with the church; we are going to continue praising and serving the Lord. However, the mistake that most of us make is in not striving for something deeper than waist-high religion.

I am not satisfied with my place in the Lord. I want to go deeper in the Spirit, deeper in the Word, deeper in faith and grace, deeper in love and in the will of God. I am glad that there is something deeper than waist-high religion. As rewarding and fulfilling as the waist-high depth in the Lord is, we can go deeper. Ezekiel came out of the water that came up to his waist, walked a little farther and then was directed by the Spirit to step into the water again. When he stepped into the water again, he discovered that the stream had become a river so deep that he could no longer walk through it. He had to give himself completely to it; he had to go with the flow; he had to swim across.

When we experience religion deep enough to swim in, we don't hold any dry areas back for ourselves. We give ourselves completely to God. We know that we are not partially cleansed or forgiven or loved, but that the blood of Jesus has sanctified and cleansed us through and through, and made us new from head to foot. Our sins are completely forgiven and our salvation completely restored. We don't become perfect, we don't stop making mistakes, but we are able to give ourselves to God as never before in spite of our errors. Our prayers truly become "Thy will be done." We recognize that, "Lord I'm not important, but your will and your work are. I just want to be an instrument in your hands."

When religion becomes deep enough to swim in, we no longer stand on our own feet, or try to walk or wade through on our own power. Instead we rely on God's Word and put our trust in God as never before. Live or die, sink or swim, we forge through life's turbulent seas believing that underneath us are everlasting arms upholding us against tempestuous waves and raging billows. With all we have—our lives, our families, our careers—we dare to swim on the care and under the protection and grace of God. When Cortez's five hundred conquistadors disembarked on the eastern coasts of Mexico, Cortez set fire to his ships. His warriors, watching their means of retreat and passage back home burning in the harbor, knew that they were committing their lives to the conquest of the new world for Spain. When our religion gets deep enough to swim in, there is no turning back; no walking away or quitting when our feeling gets hurt; no being chased away when we are talked about; no being driven away by confusion or misunderstanding; no running away when we get a preacher we don't like. We're in deep water, and we're swimming with all we have to reach the other side.

I know that religion that's deep enough to swim in can be frightening because of the commitment and daring it calls for, but that is the kind of religion that will take us through. There is a story in the annals of the British Navy about an occasion when a warship was lying in a harbor in the West Indies with five other ships from various nations. Suddenly a furious storm descended and wild, terrifying winds and great waves swept into the harbor. The British captain raised the anchor and sailed out into the sea into the very midst of the storm. Two days later he returned, battered but safe. There he saw the other ships piled up and wrecked upon the shore. It was their refusal to face the seas and the storm, their clinging to security, which had been the cause of their undoing. Only the ship that had ventured everything came through.

Only persons whose religion is deep enough so that they forsake the security of shallow waters and venture forth swimming, trusting in God's Word, depending upon God's grace, relying on God's power, will be able to come through life's storms. Persons whose religion keeps them close to the shores where water comes only to their ankles, knees or even waist, will be battered and crushed by life's storms. Only religion that's deep enough to swim in can make you more than a conqueror. How deep is your religion? Is your religion deep enough to help you pick up the pieces of your life and go on living triumphantly, even when you've lost a loved one? Is your religion deep enough to help you keep your head up when misfortune strikes and the very foundation of your life is shaken? Is your religion deep enough to keep your heart from panic and your courage from fleeing when hellhounds are on your trail trying to undermine you at every turn? And, when you come to the end of your journey, "weary of life and the battle is won," is your religion deep enough to make up a dying bed and then bear you on the wings of God's eternal morning to the bosom of your heavenly Father who will wipe all tears from your eyes and give eternal rest to your soul?

How deep is your religion?

The Dreamer

Genesis 37:14-20

I t was Joseph, one of the youngest of Jacob's twelve sons, who surprised and angered his brothers one day when he told them about two of his dreams. Joseph told his brothers, "I had a dream in which we were binding sheaves in the field when my sheaf arose and stood upright and your sheaves bowed to mine."

Naturally his brothers resented Joseph, first for the audacity of the dream, and second for his articulation of it to them. They said to him: "Shall you indeed reign or have dominion over us?"

Before Joseph's brothers could recover from the shock of his first dream he told them about the second. He said: "I had a dream in which the sun, moon and eleven stars bowed before me." This time even Joseph's father reacted and said, "Just what are you saying? Shall I, your mother and your brothers bow before you?" According to the Scriptures, Joseph's brothers hated him because of his dreams, however his father took note of them.

It was on a hot Wednesday, August 28, 1963, that Martin Luther King, Jr., standing in the twilight of the fading afternoon and in the shadow of the Lincoln Memorial in Washington, D.C., proclaimed for all America and all of the world to hear:

I still have a dream. It is a dream deeply rooted in the American dream. I have a dream that one day this nation will rise up and live out the true meaning of its creed, "We hold these truths to be self-evident: that all men are created equal; that they are endowed by their Creator with certain inalienable rights; that among these are life, liberty, and the pursuit of happiness." I have a dream that one day on the red hills of Georgia, sons of former slaves and sons of former slave owners will be able to sit down together at the table of brotherhood. I have a dream that one day even the state of Mississippi—a state sweltering with the heat of injustice, sweltering with the heat of oppression—will be transformed into an oasis of freedom and justice. I have a dream that my four little children will one day live in a nation where they will not be judged by the color of their skin but by the content of their character. I have a dream today. I have a dream that one day down in Alabama with its vicious racists, with its governor having his lips dripping with words of "interposition" and "nullification," one day right there in Alabama little black boys and girls will be able to join hands with little white boys and girls as sisters and brothers. I have a dream today. I have a dream that one day every valley shall be exalted, every hill and mountain shall be made low, the rough places will be made plain, and the crooked places will be made straight, and the glory of the Lord shall be revealed, and all flesh shall see it together.[1]

"Well now," Joseph's brothers asked, "what do you do about a little brother who has gotten out of line? We can't discredit him with Father, for the more we try to do to him, the more protective of him Father becomes. The last time we told a lie to him about Joseph, Father went out and brought him a multicolored coat. What do you do about a little brother who dares to make himself our equal and even our superior?"

On the evening of August 28, 1963, America was also faced with a series of perplexing questions. What do you do *about* a black man and his dreams? What do you do *with* a black man who dares to articulate his dreams and aspirations? What do you do *to* a black man who dreams about equality and a reversal of the whole social and political order—who talks about exalting valleys, levelling hills, and straightening out the crooked places? What kind of response do you make to him and to his dreams?

Joseph's brothers said, "Let us attack; let us kill; let us destroy the dreamer. And then, let us tell a lie to cover up what we've done. Let's tell Father that a wild beast has devoured him. And after we've disposed of the dreamer, then 'we shall see what will become of his dreams.' "

There were those in America whose responses to King was to attack. There were those who said, "Let us destroy the dreamer. We will destroy him by discrediting him. We will discredit him first with his family, by spreading all kinds of rumors and gossip about his personal and moral life. We will send his wife a spurious and unclear tape on which she will hear his voice, supposedly, talking about one of his alleged affairs. We will discredit him with the black community by calling him a thief. We will tell the people that he is stealing their money and turning in fraudulent income tax returns. There are always those who are open to, ready, and willing to receive that kind of gossip. Then we will discredit him with white America by calling him a Communist. Most whites don't understand him and don't know how to cope with him anyway. There are always some who will believe any kind of lie, tale, rumor, or superstition we circulate about blacks. So let's destroy his credibility first. And if that doesn't work let us slay the dreamer himself, and cover what we've done by withholding evidence and telling more lies. Then 'we shall see what will become of his dreams.' "

Perhaps there was one in the group who said, "Well, maybe we're getting too worked up about Joseph and his dream. Just because somebody dreams something doesn't mean it has to come true. After all, dreams can be fantasy. Let him go ahead and dream. After all, when Father dies we will be in charge. We are still the elder brothers and there is no way he can jump over all of us and become the head of the family."

There were those who regarded King's dreams as fantasy. Governor Ross Barnett of Mississippi; Senator Richard Russell of Georgia; Senator Strom Thurmond of South Carolina; Public Safety Director of Birmingham, Bull Connors; Sheriff

Jim Clark of Selma; Governor George Wallace of Alabama; J. Edgar Hoover of the F.B.I.—had they been listening, I'm sure they would have told King that he was fantasizing and out of his mind to believe that such a dream could ever come to pass in America. They probably said, "The 'nigras' have had their field day in Washington. They've had a good shout and a big picnic and can go on home now believing that they've made some progress, and we can get back to doing business as usual in America."

However, a few years later, when I saw a picture of George Wallace crowning the first black queen of the University of Alabama from his wheelchair—when just a few years before he had so boldly stood on his feet to defy the mandate from the high court of the land to block the entrance of the first two black students to that school—it let me know that God does have a way of making the wildest dreams become realities, when they are given from and by heaven.

A few years later, when I saw Strom Thurmond campaigning for black votes in South Carolina, I was reminded again that God still has a way of levelling hills and exalting valleys.

A few years later, when I saw Jim Clark voted out of office by black voters, I was reminded that God can still bring down the mighty and exalt the lowly.

A few years later, when this country observed the birthday of Dr. Martin Luther King, Jr.—not J. Edgar Hoover or Bull Connors—as a national holiday, I was reminded again that God can still make the first last and the last first.

Reuben said, "Let's not kill him; let's defer him." The others said: "Let's sell him into slavery, and file him away in that part of the memory bank labelled deferred and forgotten. And then we will see what will become of his dreams."

While some attacked the dreamer and his dreams, while some dismissed them as fantasy, others simply filed them away. They simply begged off "the Negro question" and deferred the dream. They put it in the hands of the committee on "benign neglect" and left it there. They told black America, "We are too involved with too many other issues of national

import; we've got a war to fight in Vietnam; we don't have time
to be bothered with you."

But what happens to a dream deferred? The great black
bard, Langston Hughes once asked:

> What happens to a dream deferred?
> Does it dry up like a raisin in the sun
> Or fester like a sore and then run
> Does it stink like rotten meat
> Or crust and sugar over like syrupy sweet
> Does it sink like a heavy load
> Or does it explode?[2]

What does deferment do to the dreamer, and how does it
affect the dream? Dreams can turn into nightmares. Everyone
knows about King's speech at the March on Washington but
not a whole lot of us have taken time to read *The Trumpet of
Conscience*, where King wrote:

> . . . I must confess to you today that not long after talking about
> that dream I started seeing it turn into a nightmare . . . I remem-
> ber the first time that I saw that dream turn into a nightmare,
> just a few weeks after I had talked about it. It was when four
> beautiful, unoffending Negro girls were murdered in Birming-
> ham, Alabama. I watched that dream turn into a nightmare as I
> moved through the ghettoes of the nation and saw my black
> brothers and sisters perishing on a lonely island of poverty in
> the midst of a vast ocean of material prosperity, and saw the
> nation doing nothing to grapple with the Negroes' problem of
> poverty. I saw that dream turn into a nightmare as I watched my
> black brothers and sisters in the midst of anger and understand-
> able outrage . . . turn to misguided riots to try to solve that
> problem.[3]

Did the system finally beat King? Did the attacks kill the
dreamer and did the deferment plan kill the dream? The
answer to that question is an emphatic and resounding No!
King goes on to state:

> Yes, I am personally the victim of deferred dreams, of blasted
> hopes, but in spite of that I close today saying I still have a
> dream, because you know you can't give up on life. If you lose

hope, somehow you lose that vitality that keeps life moving, you lose that courage to be, that quality that helps you to go on in spite of all. And so today I still have a dream.[4]

Joseph's brothers made a big mistake. They assumed that Joseph was the source of the dream. They didn't understand that Joseph didn't make that dream up in his head, but that it was put there by somebody else—somebody bigger than Joseph, his brothers, Pharaoh, and Egypt. They didn't understand that the Maker and Giver of the dream never took his hand off Joseph's life. They didn't know that the dream-Giver was using their evil designs and that a lie told by the wife of an Egyptian official and a nightmare given to a king would be used to bring about the fulfillment of Joseph's dream. They didn't know that God was using their evil to fortify Joseph and his faith for that moment when Joseph's brothers would come to his doorstep begging bread.

I can see Joseph as he smiled at them, not a smirk of "Now's my chance to get even"; not a sarcastic grin of "I showed them"; not a gloating look of victory—but a smile of thanksgiving and satisfaction that somehow through it all he had been kept by divine power.

Because he had waited on God, he had been allowed to see the goodness of the Lord in the land of the living. Because he had trusted the God who gave him his dream, that same God had taken those same dreams that people said could and would never be and brought them to fruition. That same God had taken those same dreams that folk said he was uppity for dreaming and had no right to dream and turned them into living realities. I can see Joseph as he looked at his brothers and said, "You meant it for evil, but God meant it for good."

What happens when a dreamer is attacked and his dream deferred? I'll tell you what happens. The same God who gave the dream uses those hardships and evil acts which were meant to destroy God's servants as a means for fortifying and strengthening the dreamer.

What King was saying when he talked about believing in his dream in spite of nightmarish realities is the same thing that the church at Corinth, and every black person who has struggled and met disappointments and still gone on to victory, has said: "We are troubled on every side, yet not distressed; we are perplexed, but not in despair; persecuted, but not forsaken; cast down, but not destroyed" (2 Corinthians 4:8-9, KJV). His body could be killed but neither King nor the dream itself could be destroyed because King had learned to trust the God of Joseph, the God of his mother and father, the God who had set his soul on fire and told him, 'I have set thee a watchman on the wall' " (Ezekiel 3:17, KJV).

King, like Paul, learned that in all things God's grace is still sufficient and God's strength is made perfect in weakness. King knew that no matter what people said about him or did to him he could not be discredited with his heavenly Father, who had put on his back the multicolored robe of mercy, redemption, salvation, love, and forgiveness which had been purchased by the blood of Jesus on Calvary.

What happens when the dreamer is attacked and his dream deferred? If you trust God, he will let you see the fulfillment of your dreams. It was in Memphis, Tennessee, when he was in one of the toughest struggles of his career, that King talked about another dream, another vision. He said: "We've got some difficult days ahead. But it really doesn't matter to me now because I've been to the mountaintop . . . Like anybody, I would like to live a long life . . . But I'm not concerned about that now. I just want to do God's will. And He's allowed me to go up to the mountain. And I've looked over and I've seen the promised land. I may not get there with you, but I want you to know tonight that we as a people will get to the promised land . . . 'Mine eyes have seen the glory of the coming of the Lord.' "

God's One

Luke 17:11-19

In Luke 17:11-19, we read that Jesus healed ten "untouchables"—ten lepers. This incident is not only another example of the healing power of Christ, it is a demonstration of the Master's sensitivity to human need and his ever-present compassion.

The sight of lepers was common in Jesus' day and most people grew accustomed to seeing them. Suffering and misery are like anything else—we can get used to them. If we see them enough, if we're confronted by them enough, then we cease to be shocked by them and we learn to accept them as the natural order of things.

However, Jesus was not so accustomed to suffering and misery and tragedy that he could take problems, injustices, and pain lightly. Whenever he saw misery, something moved within him; his heart was touched and he responded. He knew that he couldn't heal everybody in the world but that didn't stop him from healing those that he could. Thus, when the lepers cried out to him, Jesus responded.

As the lepers followed Jesus' command to go show themselves to the priest, they found themselves cleansed. As they followed the instructions of Jesus, they found themselves healed. It came to pass that as they went, they were cleansed. Deliverance, cleansing, salvation, and healing come to us only as we listen to the directives of the Lord and obey. Sometimes those directives may seem strange, but it is only as we trust and obey; it is only as we, in faith, venture to do as the Lord has commanded and the Spirit has directed, that we are set free from that which once held us bound.

When the lepers discovered their healing, what was their response? Nine went their way, while one returned to give thanks. When the one returned, glorifying God for what had been done in his life, Jesus asked, "Didn't I heal ten? Where are the nine?" I don't know exactly where the other nine went, but if you allow me to use my imagination, I'll tell you why I think they might not have returned to give thanks.

Perhaps a couple of them didn't return because they took their healing for granted. There was no reason to be thankful because they felt that they had been given a raw deal in life. The disease had been unfairly thrust upon them, so the healing was only what they deserved. They were embittered about their condition and, because their bitterness was so deep, they were not particularly thankful for their relief.

There are many people in life who feel that the world owes them a living; they take the blessings that God gives them for granted. When we think of the unemployed, the destitute, and the hungry, what makes us think that we are any more deserving of the jobs we have, or the food on our tables, or the shelter above our heads, than anyone else? If we have been blessed, it's not because we have an inherent right or that we are deserving. There are a lot of deserving people who don't have what we have. We have been blessed because God is good and has chosen to bless us.

Six girls sat down in a cafeteria. One bowed her head to say grace while the others snickered. She asked them why they were laughing and why didn't they, too, give thanks. "For what?" they answered, "We paid for the food." "Where did you get the money?" she asked. "Family," was the reply. "Where did they get it?" the girl asked. "Worked for it," they answered. "Where did they get the strength to go to work— where does it all come from?" the praying girl asked. The next day, all six girls said grace when they sat down to eat.

What I am saying is that every good and perfect gift comes from above. So instead of taking life for granted, we should live life in gratitude.

There are some church people who feel that if things go right in the church: "It's what we did," but if things go wrong: "It's what the Reverend did." Some people feel that when something good comes their way: "It's what I did, what I worked for; it's my accomplishment." But the minute something bad happens, our tune becomes: "Why did God do this to me; why did God let this happen to me; why is God so hard on me?"

But when we approach life with an attitude of gratitude, we give thanks in all things. Like Habakkuk, we can say, "Although the fig tree shall not blossom, neither shall fruit be in the vines, the labor of the olive shall fail, and the fields yield not meat; the flock shall be cut off from the fold, and there shall be no herd in the stall, yet I will rejoice in the Lord, I will joy in the God of my salvation" (Habakkuk 3:17-18, KJV).

Not all of the lepers took their healing for granted. Some were grateful and they meant to return to say thank-you to Jesus, but they became sidetracked and never got around to it. They meant to return to Jesus just as soon as they left the temple. But they decided to go home first and show themselves to their families. They decided to go by the old neighborhood and see their old friends, as well as some of the people who had shunned them before.

When they went home they started celebrating and before they knew it the day was gone and the night was gone. Before they knew it a week was gone, a month was gone, a year was gone. Before they knew it Jesus was gone. Before they knew it Jesus had been crucified, and they never got around to thanking him.

They didn't do it purposefully; they had the best of intentions. They meant to thank him; they just became so engrossed in their own agendas, they got so caught up in their own celebrations, they just never got around to it.

There are a lot of people who will end up in hell because of "meant to" religion. We *meant to* visit the sick; we *meant to* ask our neighbors' forgiveness; we *meant to* say a kind word. We *meant to* go to church; we certainly *meant to* keep all those promises we made when we were sick. We *meant to* be a good Christian husband or wife, son or daughter, father or mother—but we just became sidetracked.

We became so engrossed in doing what we wanted to do that we kept putting it off. Then we looked around and our opportunities were gone. The best years of our lives were gone; our children were grown; the person we intended to be reconciled with was gone—but we *meant to* do it.

"Meant to" religion has never done anything but talk. It has never saved a soul, comforted the sick, or repaired any hurt feelings. That's why we must act whenever we get the chance.

We used to sing, "I believe I'll testify while I have a chance, for I may not have this chance anymore." So let us act when we have a chance. The writer says, "Today when you hear my voice harden not your heart" (Hebrews 4:17). Longfellow wrote:

> Trust no future however pleasant
> Let the dead past bury its dead
> Act, act within the living present
> Heart within and God o'erhead.

The one grateful leper had to turn back and retrace his steps to get to Jesus. Perhaps the others were grateful, but they didn't feel like going through the trouble of turning back to give thanks. They found it much easier to go on their merry way. To find Jesus they would have had to return to the spot and revisit those same places where they were once lepers. They wanted to forget all about that and so they just continued on their journey.

It's easier to continue on our way than to pause and do a little backtracking to give thanks. It takes a little extra effort on our part to give thanks. It's easier to lay in bed on Sunday morning or wash the car or relax around the house than it is to get dressed and go to church to thank and praise God for last week's journey. It's easier to stay at home in the kitchen or in front of the television on Thanksgiving Day than it is to get up and go out to church to say, "I thank you, Jesus, for what you've done for me."

It's easy to get so involved in our activities that we can't find the time to serve God. Some of us don't want to think about the time when we were outcasts, when we didn't have much of anything, before the hand of the Lord rescued us. Some of us are so far on our way that we think it's too much to retrace our steps back to Jesus. It's easier to just go on our way.

Yes, the vast majority of people, for one reason or another, fail to give God proper thanks. Jesus asked, "Didn't I heal ten? Where are the nine?" Ten were healed but only one returned, but thank God for the one. No matter how bad things may get, no matter how many turn their backs on God, someone will return to give thanks.

I've found out, as a preacher, that when things get rough and supporters are few, God always sends someone to offer a word of encouragement. God always has one who says, "Reverend, I'm praying for you. Reverend, I'll do what I can. Reverend, I'm with you. I can't speak for the others, but you can count on me."

God always has one. That one's name may be Noah, Abraham, Moses; it may be Joshua, Gideon, or Esther; it may be Elijah, Isaiah, or Jeremiah; it may be Daniel, or John the Baptist, or Stephen, or Paul, or John of Patmos; it may be Richard Allen, or Harriet Tubman, or Martin Luther King, Jr., but God always has somebody. Sometimes God has more than we think; Elijah found that out on Mount Horeb when he thought he was the only one.

Jesus asked, "Didn't I heal ten men? Where are the nine? Does only this foreigner return to give glory to God?" Among the ten lepers there was one who was a despised Samaritan. There was one who was not only the victim of leprosy, but he was also the victim of intense prejudice and hatred from the Jews. Yet when the healing took place, it was the Samaritan who returned to give thanks. Jesus' own people went on their way. It was one who was considered a foreigner, the one we would least expect, who came back shouting, "Glory to God, I've been healed."

Many times God's choice is the one that we would consider to be the least likely. When God got ready for a deliverer for the children of Israel, God picked the world's most unlikely candidate: Moses. A son of Pharaoh's court, Moses was a former general of the Egyptian army and a murderer who spoke with a stammer. When Samuel went to Jesse's house, God chose David, the youngest of Jesse's sons, who was only a shepherd boy and who was the least likely candidate to be a king over Israel.

When God was ready for an apostle to the Gentiles he got the one least likely: Saul, a zealous Pharisee and ardent persecutor of the church. That's why, from the youngest to the oldest, we have to treat everyone right. Jesus says, "Whoever receives a little child in my name receives me; and whoever receives me, receives not me but him who sent me. . . . Whoever causes one of these little ones who believe in me to sin, it would be better for him if a great millstone were hung round his neck and he were thrown into the sea" (Mark 9:37, 42). Jesus says, "Inasmuch as ye have done it to the least; you have done it unto me" (Matthew 25:40, KJV).

The very person we mistrust or abuse may be the one who is walking closest to God. In the church, God's anointed is not always the one with the biggest mouth or the highest office. God's person is not always the individual who is up front all the time or the one who gives the most. God's person may not say much and may not even get any recognition. They may not even hold an office, but that's alright because God knows who these persons are. Their souls have been set free and their names have been written in the Lamb's book of life.

Jesus was thanked by the one least likely. Often our blessings come not from those we've helped the most, but from those about whom we have not given much thought. Often those for whom we don't think we've done very much are the most appreciative. Maybe what we did was a little thing to us, but it was a big thing to them. That's what makes doing good worthwhile. The nine may go their own way, never bothering to say thank you, never thinking about how we've helped them or what we've tried to do for them. But when the one comes back, we know the kindness we've tried to do has not been in vain. Let us not become discouraged over the nine; just thank God that we've been able to help the one.

I don't know about you, but this is how I approach life. I may not be able to sing like angels; I may not be able to preach like Paul; I may not be rich or smart; history books may never record my works, but if in the course of this life I've been able to help one person, then everything's all right. If one person has been brought closer to God; if one young person has been guided in the right way; if one old person has been comforted in their loneliness; if one sick person has been helped to hold on until deliverance comes; if one soul has been saved; if one life has been redeemed; if one person has seen the beauty of Jesus shining through my wretched life, then my living has not been in vain.

> If I can help somebody as I pass along,
> If I can cheer somebody with a word or song,
> If I can show somebody that they're traveling
>   wrong.
> Then my living shall not be in vain.[1]

The Gift That Counts

Acts 1:12–14

Acts 1:12-14 describes the ascension of Jesus. This is the last time that Mary, the mother of Jesus, is mentioned in the Scriptures. In this passage we see her, along with the brothers of Jesus, continuing in fellowship with the disciples and other members of the early church.

The Gospel of Luke tells us that the disciples returned from the mount of ascension with joy, unlike the first time that Jesus left them, when their hearts were broken. Although they were sad to see him go, they were still joyful because the second departure was one of victory rather than defeat. It was one of glory rather than shame, exaltation rather than condemnation, power rather than weakness, and divinity rather than humanity. They had seen Jesus in his lowest hour and, because they loved him, they had to rejoice on the day of his ascension and exaltation, even though he was leaving them.

If the Day of Ascension meant much to the disciples, it must have meant more than words could explain to Mary, Jesus' mother. We often speak about the unsettling effect of Jesus' ministry upon his disciples and friends. To them, he was at times an enigma whom they never completely understood or quite figured out. We often talk about the devastating effect of the crucifixion of Jesus upon his disciples and friends without realizing that, whatever they went through, the impact was even more confusing and painful to Mary, Jesus' mother. After all, they had only known Jesus for three-and-a-half years at the most, while Mary had known him longer than any other human being on earth. She was the vessel whom the Holy Spirit blessed to bring forth God's Son. Mary was the first human being to receive the word from heaven that a Saviour would be born.

It was Mary, who under the power of the Holy Spirit, felt the first stirrings of the Saviour's life within her body. It was Mary who carried the child during pregnancy, loving the life within but not understanding exactly what had happened to her or the nature or role of the baby which she bore. It was Mary who personally experienced the pain and joy of childbirth as her baby was brought forth in very mean and crude circumstances—in a stable behind an overcrowded inn in an overcrowded city where nobody seemed to care or take notice. She had been with Jesus at the very first moment of his earthly life.

She had been there when shepherds came to see her baby, bringing strange reports about heavenly hosts proclaiming glad hosannas to a newborn Saviour. She had been there when gift-bearing wise men came from the East with a strange story of following an unusually bright star which had led them to the holy family. She had seen both the shepherds and the wise men bow down to worship her child. She did not understand the meaning of those events but she kept them in her heart. Sometimes the meaning of life's events are not immediately revealed to us; we must keep them stored in our hearts until a later time.

Only Mary could remember the day she took the baby to be dedicated in the temple. Only Mary could remember Simeon, who, desiring before his death to see the Messiah, glorified God as he laid his eyes on the child. Only Mary could remember how perplexed and startled she felt when Simeon told her that, because of the role her son would play in the redemption of Israel, a sword would pierce her own soul as well.

She could remember the initial pain from that sword when Joseph awoke her one night and told her to pack their belongings quickly because they had to flee to Egypt, for King Herod wanted to destroy their child. Only Mary could remember the fear in her heart as she and Joseph fled that night and as she wondered why anyone would want to destroy her precious baby.

She could remember the relief she and Joseph felt when they received word from heaven that they could return to their homeland, and their excitement when they finally settled in Nazareth. Mary could remember her parental anxiety the time they had gone to a feast in Jerusalem and assumed that Jesus was returning with some of their relatives, only to discover after traveling for a whole day, that their son had been left in the city. Only Mary could remember how she had worried as she stopped strangers, went to the houses of friends and relatives, and searched Jerusalem until she found her child in the temple. When she told him that she and his father had been worried sick about him, she felt a bit of the sword again when he revealed to her that he already had a dawning awareness of a special destiny. How could she ever forget his answer, "How is it that you sought me? Did you not know that I must be in my Father's house about my Father's business?" (Luke 2:49).

Mary could remember the joys of those Nazareth days as Jesus increased in wisdom and in stature and in favor with God and people. Mary had watched him mature into manhood and take up the tools of carpentry—his earthly father's profession. However, she had not forgotten the visits of the shepherds and wise men in his infancy, nor his answer that day in the temple. She knew that there would come a time when he would leave Nazareth.

Mary tried to prepare herself for the inevitable. However, she would never forget the pain of that day when Jesus tenderly informed her that he had to leave home and pursue the calling he felt within.

Only a parent can understand how Mary fought back tears and forced a smile as she stood in the cottage door saying goodbye to her oldest son and watching him walk down the road until he was out of sight. Only a parent knows how much she worried and how much she wondered what would happen to her child. Only a parent knows how hard she prayed that night and every night and morning thereafter that the God who gave him to her would watch over her child and protect him from hurt, harm, and danger.

Mary could remember when she began to receive mixed reports about her son's ministry. Some said that he did mighty works for God while others said he was crazy. She could remember how upset their neighbors, friends, and relatives had been when he returned to Nazareth in an attempt to do there what he had done elsewhere. She could remember the pain and sorrow in his eyes when his message and ministry had been rejected. She could remember how he looked at her when he said, "A prophet is not without honor, except in his own country, and among his own kin, and in his own house" (Mark 6:4).

After Jesus left Nazareth, she continued to fear the worst might be true—her son was being driven by some evil spirit which was not of this world. With one of his brothers, she had sought him out that she might bring him home for a much-needed rest. She was, however, to learn the painful lesson that when God is working with a person not even the nearest and dearest of kin has the right to interfere.

Mary had to learn that human beings must be careful about reaching hasty conclusions when God is working with or through someone. Mary had to learn that God's work, God's plan, God's timetable, all defy human judgment. As one writer said:

> Judge not the Lord by feeble sense,
> Nor scorn his work in vain;
> God is his own interpreter,
> And He will make it plain.

One day Mary received the news that Jesus had been arrested in Jerusalem and would probably be put to death. She left home immediately in order to be near her son. No matter what the world said about him, he was still her son. Irrespective of what he had or had not done, he was still her son. Irrespective of whether he was possessed with the spirit of God or an evil spirit, whether he was in his right mind or not, he was still her son. Although he was a condemned criminal and despite the disgrace and shame of the crucifixion, he was still her son. She saw him struggle under the weight of the cross and she saw him stumble and fall. How she wanted to run to him and lift the cross from his shoulders, but she couldn't; he had to bear his own cross.

When my own children are ill, how I wish I could take their fever and bear their pain, but I can't. Each of us must bear our own crosses and experience our own pain. Every lash Jesus received was a lash across Mary's heart. Each blow of the hammer that drove the nails deeper into his hands and feet—those hands and feet that she had washed and held when he was a child—was felt within her soul. Every drop of blood shed was as her own because that person on the cross was not just some misguided prophet or criminal, that suffering mass of humanity was flesh of her flesh and bone of her bone.

That's why she stood near the cross. Others might sit and watch with complacency. Others might curse him, or mock and laugh. Others might hide their faces in shame or stand afar off. But Mary was bold enough to stand near the cross where her son—her little boy, her growing teenager, her young man—was dying. She had been with him at the beginning; she would be with him at the end. When he hung his head and died, part of her spirit died with him.

Others may have had their grief but her's was special—her's was a mother's grief. It was the grief of one who had carried him in her womb, gone through the travail of birth, nursed him, cared for him, taught and guided him, and one who had prayed a mother's prayer for him.

When Jesus ascended into heaven, Mary had a special joy. No one had been with him as long as she had. No one had prayed for him like she had. No one had loved him as long or suffered as she had.

Ascension Day for Mary was Mother's Day. On that day the

plan of salvation that had begun over thirty-three years, before when the angel Gabriel had visited her, was brought to a glorious finale. On that day she received the ultimate gift—the gift that counts. It was the gift of knowing that her faithfulness, labor, pain, love, and prayers had not been in vain.

Jesus was now the ascended, exalted and reigning Lord of all nations; the conqueror of every foe. The life which she had brought into the world now held the keys to eternal life in his hand. She who had been a lowly peasant girl, she who had been the least, had brought forth the most—the fairest of ten thousand.

On Mother's Day we take the time to do special things. We send cards, buy or cook dinners, and purchase special gifts. But if we really want to give a gift—either to one who is dead or to someone who is with us still—give a gift that counts. Give a life that amounts to something. Give a life that says to those whom we honor that their labor, love, prayer, teaching, and sacrifices have not been in vain.

It is said that the famed songstress, Marian Anderson, was once asked what was her greatest moment. The reporter knew that she had a number of great moments to choose from—she had sung in private audiences before the Roosevelts at the White House; she had sung privately before the King and Queen of England; she had received the ten-thousand-dollar Bok award as the person who had done the most for Philadelphia, her hometown. However, Marian Anderson chose none of these moments but said, "The greatest moment in my life was the day I went home and told my mother that she wouldn't have to take in washing any more."

Whether honoring a mother living or dead, we can give a gift that counts. We can give the gift of a life that counts: a life that has been set free by Jesus and surrendered to his will; a life that has found its way back to the church where it was nurtured; a life that's determined not to let Satan and sin be in control; a life that says, "If the Lord wants somebody, here am I, send me. I'll go!" We can give a life that says to living mothers, "Hold your head up, everything's going to be all right." We can give a life that says to mothers who have gone home to glory, "Sleep on and take your rest, for your living has not been in vain."

Give a gift that counts. Give fruits of repentance. Give flowers of a life that is abloom with God's grace, Jesus' love, and the Holy Spirit's comfort. Send a greeting that says your name has been recorded in the Lamb's book of life. Give a gift that counts. Come back home, not only to a mother's embrace but to God's mercy, Jesus' salvation, and the Holy Spirit's anointing.

We Are God's Children

1 John 3:1-2

There are some great lessons and truths in life that we must never allow ourselves to forget. There are some things we must hold onto, no matter what. To be sure, there are some things that are not worth the effort of remembering: the petty, the mundane, the garbage we hear about ourselves and the gossip we hear about others. These are the kinds of things that we would be helped by forgetting. These things add nothing substantive to our character, nor do they help us to really appreciate others.

Yet these are the things that most of us are inclined to remember and most prone to repeat. There are those who delight in making up and/or carrying tales about others. There are those who delight in reciting a list of woes and personal injuries. These persons often feel sorry for themselves. When we feel sorry for ourselves it is difficult if not impossible to live a productive life. Consequently, these people who are doing nothing use what has happened in the past to justify what they are not doing now.

There are those who major in trivia. Trivia is information which can be interesting, but which could just as easily be forgotten and the world would go on without missing it. Gossip, the mundane, our personal catalogue of misfortunes, and sob stories can be interesting. That's why they are repeated so often with so much zest. However, whether they are worth remembering is another issue. Everything that is interesting might not be worth remembering. Whether our minds and time might be better used concentrating on some other things is another issue.

There are some other truths in life that are worth remembering. They are the things that really matter in the long run. When personal tragedies, illnesses, or setbacks in careers shake the foundations of our lives; when we are faced with mountains that seem insurmountable and rivers that seem uncrossable; when we have more problems than solutions and more dilemmas than answers; when we believe that we have hit life's rock bottom, these are the experiences that shake us out of our lethargy and aid us in the renewing of our strength. For peace of mind, for the renewing of our spirits, the strengthening of our soul, the edification of faith, and the undergirding of courage, I submit the truth that we are God's children.

No matter what happens to us in life, one truth that we must never allow ourselves to forget is that we are God's children. In reflecting upon the truth of this assertion, the writer of the First Epistle of John has stated, in our text: "See what love the Father has given us, that we should be called children of God; and so we are. The reason why the world does not know us that is it did not know him. Beloved, we are God's children now; it does not yet appear what we shall be, but we know that when he appears we shall be like him, for we shall see him as he is" (1 John 3:1-2).

Now when the writer refers to God as father, he is not being sexist or noninclusive in his language but is describing a kind of relationship that humanity can have with divinity. The writer is saying that the relationship between God and us is closer than the bond between Creator and creature or master and servant; it is analogous to that of parent and child.

Parents and children are united in a way that is distinct from even husband and wife. In marriage the two become one; however, with parent and child the two were originally one, for the child is flesh of the parents' flesh and bone of the parents' bones. No generation gaps, no legal decrees, no annulments or arguments, no disappointments or failures can erase the fact that our parents and children are related in a special way.

In describing the difference between God as Father and God as Creator, Barclay has observed that the two words, "paternity" and "fatherhood," though closely related, have two widely divergent meanings. Paternity describes a relationship in which a father is responsible for the physical existence of a child; but that's where the responsibility begins and ends. After the child is born, the father need assume no responsibility for the nurture and care of that child. Fatherhood, on the other hand, describes an intimate relationship—one of love, care, and concern. Consequently, when the writer refers to God as Father, he is talking about more than God as Creator; he is talking about God as Protector, Provider, Refuge and Help in trouble; as Counsellor, as Friend.

Most importantly, the writer is talking about God as love. For fatherhood is not only about discipline and being a provider; it is also about love. It is love that makes a father feel his responsibility. It is love that inspires a father to do what he does.

The writer of First John said: "See what *love* the Father has given us, that we should be called the children of God." We are created by virtue of God's power, but it is God's love that allows us as sinful creatures and as imperfect humanity to receive the privilege of adoption as God's children.

A loving relationship is a two-way street. For it to really work, there has to be a response to the love initiative. As it is love that separates fatherhood from paternity or God the Father from God the Creator, so it is our love response that finalizes the adoption process. It is only as we respond to God's love with our life and devotion that we truly become children of God. We are all created by God and God loves each and every one of us, but only those who truly love the Lord are privileged to be called children of God.

Having God as a father means that we have a noble heritage, a meaningful present, and an even more glorious future.

In America we tend to put more emphasis on one's ethnic identity than it rightfully deserves.

In the 1960's, when I was maturing into young manhood, a number of blacks began raising questions about their historical and family roots. Because of the way slavery had cut us off from our roots in Africa and disrupted the continuity of family life, a number of blacks were saying that, historically, they really didn't know who they were. That's why the members of the Nation of Islam or the Black Muslims used an X as their last name. They said they did not know their true African names, only their American names—which were often slavemasters' surnames and which they rejected. So the X stands for our unknown past or for a past lost in history.

There are still a number of us trying to figure out who we are as an ethnic minority, as women, as handicapped persons, or as men. However, the word that comes to us from Scripture is that we have an identity that is basic and greater than any category we could name—we are God's children.

We need not feel lost historically, sociologically, psychologically, or any other way when we know that foremost and basically we are children of God. We have a heritage that goes back farther than slavery, farther than cultural biases, further than Africa, further than human history itself. We have a heritage that no middle passage can destroy. We are God's children. We were not made in the image of apes but in the image of God. We were not made to be hewers of wood and drawers of water, but were made a little lower than the angels and crowned with glory and honor. We may not know who we are historically but we know who we are essentially; we are God's children. We may not know our historical fathers, but we know our eternal Father whose name is God.

Not only do we have a noble heritage, we have a significant present. The writer of First John says, "We are God's children now." As God's children we often live with the tension between the promise and present. All of the promises in God's Word do not come to us immediately. We must wait in faith in hope to receive some things. However, there are some privileges we can enjoy now, and being a child of God is one of them. We don't have to wait for the Supreme Court to rule on our adoption or our citizenship in the kingdom; we are God's children now. We don't have to wait for society to adopt a more liberal attitude toward our condition or race or sex; we are God's children now. Whether the Constitution or Bill of Rights says it or not, whether others recognize it or not makes no difference; in God's Word it clearly states we are God's children now.

"Well if I am God's child, why am I in the shape I'm in? Why has God allowed certain things to happen to me?"

I don't know why God allows some things to happen. I just know that, in spite of those things, God the Father will love us; in spite of those things our heavenly Parent gives us strength to make it through and to overcome.

If we are making it, it is not solely through our own strength and determination. Others who have been just as able have been broken by fewer pressures than we are facing. If we are making it, it is because God has given us grace that is sufficient for and more powerful than any cross, strength that is perfected in weakness, peace that passeth understanding, and "the earnest of the Spirit" (2 Corinthians 5:5, KJV).

Being God's child doesn't mean that we don't have problems but that we can live courageously and triumphantly, as more than conquerors in the midst of all life's problems and conflicts. I know that the One who loved us so much that the Only Begotten was freely given up for our sakes will also freely give us all things. I know that "all things work together for good for them that love the Lord [or in other words to God's children], to those who are called according to [God's] purposes" (Romans 8:28, KJV).

I know that, as our text reminds us, if the world did not know him, it will not know us. As God's children we reflect the life of the Only Begotten who spoke the truth and was lied about, who did good and was persecuted, who stood for right and was crucified. But early that third morning, while it was yet dark, God raised him to stoop no more—with power, all power in his hands, because it was not possible for death to hold him and the grave to keep him any longer.

It is Christ's resurrection that gives us hope for our own victorious futures. As God's children, we are not only heirs to a noble heritage and participants in a significant present, we also anticipate a glorious future. "Beloved, we are God's children now; it does not yet appear what we shall be, but we know that when he appears we shall be like him, for we shall see him as he is" (1 John 3:2).

We don't know all that our future holds, but this much we know, that like our past and our present, it holds Jesus. We don't know all that we shall behold, but this much we know, we shall see Jesus.

We shall see Jesus not as he was, but as he is. When he was on earth, Jesus was in the image of man, but we shall see him as he is—in the glory of God. When he was on earth he was time-bound and death-eligible, but we shall see him as he is— "the first born from the dead" (Colossians 1:18). When he was on earth he was despised and rejected, but we shall see him as he truly is—the stone which, though rejected by the builders, has become the head of the corner. When he was on earth he was a servant, but we shall see him as he is—as King of kings and Lord of lords. When he was on earth he had a body that was bruised and battered, but we shall see him as he is, with a glorified and resurrected body in which the mortal has put on immortality and the corrupt has put on the incorruptible.

When Christ was on earth he was rejected by the religious leadership, but we shall see him as he is—the bishop of our souls. When he was on earth he attempted to lead a motley group of disciples—one of whom betrayed him, one who denied him, all who deserted or failed him. But when he comes again we shall see him as he is—as the captain of the Lord's host. When he was on earth he was a victim, but we shall see him as he is in glory and power.

Not only shall we see him as he is, but God's word to us is that we shall be like him. If we love him with all of our hearts, if we have suffered with him, if we have been persecuted because of him, if we have remained firm and steadfast through him, if we have been saved by him; one of these days we shall reign with him.

Therefore, no matter what happens, let us never forget that we are God's children. The story is told that once during slavery a group of Northerners visiting New Orleans was watching a group of slaves wearily shuffling along the dock returning to their work. Spiritless, without hope or enthusiasm, seemingly indifferent to life itself, they were wearily dragging themselves along. But one slave, in striking contrast to the rest, with head unbowed and spirit unbroken, walked among them with the dignified bearing of a conqueror. "Who is that fellow?" someone asked, "Is he the straw boss or the owner of the slaves?" "No," came the reply, "that one just can't get it out of his head that he is the son of a king."

And so he was. He had been dragged into slavery as a small child, but he had already been taught that he was no ordinary person; he was the son of a king, and must carry himself accordingly as long as he lived. Now, after a lifetime of hardship and abuse which had broken the spirit of others, he was still the son of a king!

Life can deal us some cruel blows. But remember you are no ordinary creature. You are God's child. You are the child of the King.

One writer said:

> My Father is rich in houses and lands,
> He holdeth the wealth of the world in His
> hands!
> Of rubies and diamonds, of silver and gold,
> His coffers are full, He has riches untold.
>
> I'm a child of the King, A child of the King;
> With Jesus my Saviour, I'm a child of the King.

We Are the World—
We Are the Children

The title of this sermon is taken from a popular song. For me, as well as millions of others, this song is very special. It is special not simply because of its lyrics or melody or beat, but because it was written for a special purpose and was recorded by some special people.

This song by Michael Jackson and Lionel Richie, was written to raise money to help the millions of suffering people in Africa and the United States. Although Michael Jackson and Lionel Richie wrote it and Quincy Jones produced and conducted it, they were far from being the only artists involved in its recording. Approximately forty entertainers lent their time and talents to make this recording. The list of artists who participated is a virtual Who's Who of the contemporary entertainment industry. Harry Belafonte, Ray Charles, the Jacksons, Cyndi Lauper, Bette Midler, Willie Nelson, the Pointer Sisters, Smokey Robinson, Kenny Rogers, Diana Ross, Paul Simon, Bruce Springsteen, Tina Turner, Dionne Warwick, and Stevie Wonder are just some of the artists who blended their voices and combined their talents for this effort. So far, many millions of dollars have been raised to aid the hungry as a result of the use of this song.

Not long after the release of the album, others became involved. One day at 10:50 A.M. Eastern Standard Time, thousands of radio stations in this country and throughout the world played the recording at the same time. Consequently, wherever one turned on the dial this record was heard. In England, Europe, Asia, and other places on the globe—places of different political persuasions, with differing cultures and languages, this song was played and heard. For a few minutes, radio stations stopped competing with each other for the advertising dollar. For a few minutes radio stations put aside such concerns as ratings and share of the market. For a few minutes common people everywhere laid aside the differences which separated them as everyone who listened to the radio heard the same song, hummed the same tune and the message on behalf of the hungry was brought to them.

As I reflect on it, that was an historic moment, a great moment, a bright spot on what often appears to be a very bleak horizon. I do not know how many people heard the song, understood its message and mission, or made the appropriate financial response; I just know that for once in my lifetime there was an effort to unite people around the world—not to build up political power or to advance the self-interests and ideology of any nation or group of nations, but to build up the spirit and power of caring for those who are the have-nots.

This small effort gives me hope for the future. It is evidence that we can dare to break through the division, hostility, and suspicion which keep us apart and find unity around the plight of the poor and the suffering. It is evidence that Satan and the forces of darkness cannot and will not ultimately triumph. This effort tells me that, unlike Cain who slew his brother, some of us understand that we are keepers of our brothers and sisters. In spite of our selfishness, there is a compassion and caring deep in our souls, put there by God, which can be touched and stirred when the cause is right and just.

Like so many, I've become concerned about the prospects of a nuclear holocaust. I don't know what the future holds, but I know that I will always be able to think about a few brief minutes when the world was drawn together and history was made because a few recording artists and disc jockeys used the instruments at their disposal and their God-given talents to champion the cause of the hungry.

It wasn't the diplomats, leaders of states, or heads of the multinational corporations that united the world, even for a few minutes; it was a group of entertainers and disc jockeys. While political and corporate heads were playing their games with each other and cutting their big deals in plush offices, a group of singers in a recording studio were making a record whose proceeds would help feed the hungry. While people were going about their daily business, disc jockeys were using the airwaves to bring to whomever listened the message of the needy.

We don't generally think much of entertainers and disc jockeys. We listen to them, buy their records, attend their concerts, copy portions of their lifestyles, and laugh at their idiosyncrasies, but we don't take them seriously. They are entertainers to us—court jesters if you please—and because their lifestyles are different from ours, we regard them as curiosities, oddities, freaks. We consider them to be plastic and shallow people who live in some sort of fantasy world.

Yet their involvement with this project showed us that there is another side to them—a side which is often forgotten and lost in the glare of the lights and cameras. It is the side of compassion and caring. Let us never forget that, beyond what we see in people, there are dimensions that we don't see. We have to be careful about judging books by their covers or people by outward appearances. We have to be careful about writing people off as shallow and about assuming that they have nothing to contribute to us because of outward appearances.

There is always another side to the personality and a deeper dimension to people than what we see. Some of us would be surprised at the great insights, thoughts, and ideas that some people carry around in their heads. Some of us would be surprised at the information that some people have and the things they could teach us both about life and ourselves if we would take the time to really talk to them.

Some of our elders and some people whom we don't respect

because they don't say much, haven't survived by being stupid. People have more sense these days than we think they have. A lot of them have forgotten more than some of us will ever know. They have survived by their wits; they have been able to outmaneuver and outthink those who thought they were dumb and didn't know how to think. Any dummy can take much and do a lot with it, but it takes a brain to take a little and know how to stretch it and do a lot with that little. Anyone who is going to be successful at either leading or working with people had better not forget that there is always another side and a deeper dimension to people than what we see.

These entertainers, while having money and personal prestige, may not have real political clout and influence. They may not be in positions to either change or impact policy. However, their being shut out of the decision-making process didn't mean that they couldn't do anything. They decided to use what they had, their talents, to support a cause they cared about. And in using their talents, they not only raised money; they did what hasn't been done in modern history—for a few minutes they made it possible for people around the globe to hear the same message in song and be united around a common cause.

Never underestimate your talents or the impact those talents can have. You may not be able to do all you might desire in solving a crisis or straightening out a situation, but there is always something you can do. Never let what you cannot do stop you from doing what you can. What you can do may be small, but there is still something you can do. That's why one writer said:

> Let none hear you idly saying, "there is nothing I
>   can do,"
> While the souls of men are dying, and the Master
>   calls for you.
> Take the task He gives you gladly, Let His work your
>   pleasure be;
> Answer quickly when He calleth, "Here am I! Send me!
>   Send me!

If you really care about something, it's better to do that small something—whether it makes an obvious difference or not—than to do nothing at all. If you do whatever you can, no matter how small, you will have the comfort of being at peace with yourself and knowing that you can face God with a clear conscience.

"We Are the World" is the combined work of a number of artists, each of whom is successful in his or her own right. Each has his or her own following, but not one of them has as much success as all of them put together. Not one of them, individually, has more influence than all of them put together. Not one of them would have been heard or received like all of them together. It was the coming together of these stars which gave this record its uniqueness.

Who knows how many of them had already given personally or been involved in individual efforts to raise funds for the hungry. However, they came together for this project. They reasoned that there is strength in unity and a greater witness for good. To record this album, each of them had to submerge his or her own ego for a time.

When one is accustomed to singing solos, it's not the easiest thing to become a part of the background as someone else sings the solo. When one is accustomed to being the lead and having one's own way, it isn't easy to become part of a group process. Yet for this cause they did this. They understood that the cause was greater than their personal egos. They understood that this was not the time to star but rather the time to work together.

We Christians can learn a few things from these stars. When are we going to learn that we can do more by working with each other than against each other? When are we going to learn that we can accomplish more together than we can with everybody trying to be a star, with everybody's ego trying to outshine all others, with everybody trying to have his or her way, with everybody trying to do his or her thing for themselves, by themselves, with themselves?

When are we going to learn that the cause which we

represent—the cause of the kingdom of God—is greater than any one of us? When are we going to learn that there are some things more important than our wants, wishes, programs, opinions, and feelings? When are we going to learn that the world will be more receptive to what we say when we start showing more togetherness and cooperation among ourselves?

The world does not belong to the multinational corporations or even to the nations themselves. The world is not the private domain of the super-rich or the superpowers who use up natural resources at will and who manipulate people according to their own ambition. No, we, the people, are the world.

History may never record any of our deeds or words; yet we are the world. All of us are children in one human family whose mother and father is God. Because we are the world and all of us are God's children, we must assume our part of the responsibility for taking care of this world which belongs to God.

It's easy to criticize, but we are part of this world, this community, this church, so we need to ask, "What are we doing to make things better?" It's easy to say, "Let someone else do it," but we, as well as those "someone else's" are a part of this world. It's easy to say, "I can't do anything," but if we, as the children of God, don't stand for justice and speak for right, then who will? If the world is going to see a better day, then you and I, along with the "somebody elses," will have to bring it to pass. If we give the world, the church, or our private lives over to others, they will take them and run with them. We have to make a choice to save our own lives, for we are the world, we are the children.

I'm glad that this song talks about us in terms of children because, unlike the world, God has always found a place for the leadership of children. The world would say that children are the least-likely candidates for affecting change. No one would select or elect a child to lead a nation or a church or an army—nobody, that is, but our God.

When Eli the priest was in failing health after having served

Israel for many years, nobody would have thought about calling Samuel while he was still a child to succeed a religious leader of such long tenure—nobody but God. When Saul began to fail as Israel's king and Samuel was told to go to Jesse's house to anoint the next ruler over God's people, not even Samuel thought about calling young David, the shepherd boy, the youngest of the sons, to be Israel's next king—nobody but God. Children haven't matured and been seasoned yet and therefore to call them or anoint them too soon is risky. But God does it because God can see potential that we cannot or will not see.

God told Samuel "the Lord looks on the heart" (1 Samuel 16:7). That's why some of us have been placed in the positions we occupy. As fickle, stubborn, ornery, weak, and sinful as we are, nobody would have risked putting us in these positions but God. When the world would have written us off as nobodies with mediocre abilities, God said, "They are my children. I see something of worth in them and so, in spite of all they are not, I'm going to give them a chance."

I'm glad that this song talks about us as children, because children represent the future. And if there is anything that a humanity living under the threat of nuclear annihilation needs to hear, it is that we have a future. We not only have a past and a present but we have a future. "For the earth is [still] the Lord's and the fullness thereof, the world and they that dwell therein" (Psalm 24:1).

Children are so much associated with the future that when the prophet Isaiah talked about the future, he had to include a role for children. He said: "The wolf shall dwell with the lamb and the leopard shall lie down with the kid, and the calf and the lion and the fatling together, and a child shall lead them" (Isaiah 11:6). Never forget that as God's children we have a future, for "it doth not yet appear what we shall be, but we know when [Christ] shall appear, we shall be like him for we shall see him as he is" (1 John 3:2, KJV).

As God's children we have a future and it's in the hands of almighty God, for "Eye hath not seen nor ear heard, neither have entered the heart of man, the things which God hath prepared for them who love him" (1 Corinthians 2:9, KJV). Never forget that as God's children we are the world and we have a future.

Notes

A Strange Glory
[1]Adapted from Clarence E. Macartney, *Preaching Without Notes* (Grand Rapids: Baker Book House, 1976).

The Dreamer
[1]James Washington, ed., *Testament of Hope: The Essential Writings of Martin Luther King, Jr.* (Harper and Row, Publishers, Inc., 1986), p. 219.
[2]Langston Hughes, *Black Voices: An Anthology of Afro-American Literature*, Abraham Chapman, ed., (New York; NAL, 1968), pp. 430-431.
[3]Taken from Martin Luther King, Jr., *The Trumpet of Conscience* (New York: Harper and Row, Publishers Inc., 1968), pp. 76-78.

God's One
[1]From the song, "If I Can Help Somebody."